10 Ways to Show Respect to Your Husband

Respect Is Distinct From Love

Joshua FitzBurke

© **Copyright 2024 - All rights reserved.**

The content contained within this book may not be reproduced, duplicated or transmitted without direct written permission from the author or the publisher.

Under no circumstances will any blame or legal responsibility be held against the publisher, or author, for any damages, reparation, or monetary loss due to the information contained within this book, either directly or indirectly.

Legal Notice:

This book is copyright protected. It is only for personal use. You cannot amend, distribute, sell, use, quote or paraphrase any part, or the content within this book, without the consent of the author or publisher.

Disclaimer Notice:

Please note the information contained within this document is for educational and entertainment purposes only. All effort has been executed to present accurate, up to date, reliable, complete information. No warranties of any kind are declared or implied. Readers acknowledge that the author is not engaged in the rendering of legal, financial, medical or professional advice. The content within this book has been derived from various sources. Please consult a licensed professional before attempting any techniques outlined in this book.

By reading this document, the reader agrees that under no circumstances is the author responsible for any losses, direct or indirect, that are incurred as a result of the use of the information contained within this document, including, but not limited to, errors, omissions, or inaccuracies.

Table of Contents

INTRODUCTION 1

CHAPTER 1: ALLOW HIM TO PARENT HIS CHILDREN WITHOUT YOUR INTERVENTION 7

LET DAD DO HIS THING 7
    Differences in Parenting Styles Between Men and Women 9
    Showing Respect and Trust 18
    Letting Your Husband Lead Without the Need to Intervene 22

CHAPTER 2: SPEAK WELL OF HIM WITH OTHERS 29

PROTECT HIS REPUTATION 29
    The Power of Positive Words 34
    Building a Stronger Marriage 41

CHAPTER 3: REMEMBER THAT YOUR RELATIONSHIP WITH HIM PREDATES YOUR OBLIGATIONS TO YOUR CHILDREN—AND WILL OUTLIVE THEM, TOO 43

HOW POSITIVE SPEECH CAN BENEFIT YOUR RELATIONSHIP 43
    Keeping Your Relationship Alive While Raising Children 49
    Prioritizing Your Spousal Relationship 53

CHAPTER 4: APPRECIATE AND GIVE HIM CREDIT FOR HIS PROVISION, REGARDLESS OF HOW HE OBTAINED IT 57

SHOW APPRECIATION FOR YOUR HUSBAND'S PROVISION 57
    Strengthening Appreciation in Marriage 64
    More Strategies for Showing Gratitude 68

CHAPTER 5: STOP READING ROMANCE NOVELS 75

THE FAIRY-TALE EXPECTATIONS OF ROMANCE NOVELS 75
    The Impact of Emotional Porn 78
    Nurturing a Fulfilling Relationship 83

CHAPTER 6: POUR YOUR EFFORTS INTO YOUR HOUSE, NOT YOUR CAREER 87

BALANCING WORK AND FAMILY 94
Strengthening the Team Dynamic 98
Teamwork Makes the Marriage Work 102

CHAPTER 7: DON'T WORRY ABOUT IMPERFECTIONS IN YOUR LIFE GETTING IN THE WAY OF HAVING TIME FOR YOUR HUSBAND 109

MAKE CONNECTION AND INTIMACY A PRIORITY 115
Fostering Intimate Moments 119

CHAPTER 8: USE YOUR BODY LANGUAGE TO SHOW RESPECT 125

NONVERBAL COMMUNICATION IN MARRIAGE 128
Reciprocate Physical Responses 130
Elevating Your Husband 133
Strengthening the Hierarchical Aspect of Respect in Marriage ... 137

CHAPTER 9: DON'T INTERRUPT AND CORRECT HIM IN PUBLIC 141

SOCIAL DYNAMICS IN PUBLIC SETTINGS 144
Enhancing Respectful Communication 148

CHAPTER 10: ADORN YOURSELF FOR HIM 151

DESIRING TO PLEASE YOUR HUSBAND 152
Building Attraction and Connection 153

CONCLUSION 157

REFERENCES 161

Introduction

The premise of this book is simple: It's founded on the principle, "respect, not love." Now, as distinct as these two virtues may be, they are often used interchangeably, especially within the confines of a marriage. But this mix-up is precisely where the breakdown of many modern marriages begins, and I'm going to explain just why that is.

God told husbands to love their wives, and conversely, he told wives to respect their husbands (Ephesians 5:25 and 1 Peter 3:1). As you can imagine, there is a reason why God placed a command on husbands to love their wives instead of respect them, and that is because, for a man, respecting his wife is easier than loving her. Similarly, it's much easier for a woman to love her husband than it is for her to respect him. What is the immediate issue here? Well, it's that respect means everything to a man.

Now, there are times in a marriage when a husband loving his wife can seem like a daunting task, but God still expects him to do so unconditionally. Mirroring this, a wife also needs to learn to unconditionally respect her husband, even when he hasn't "earned it" in her eyes. Why? Because respect toward her husband is also something that is commanded by God.

It's no secret that the entire world, regardless of social status or religious belief, is experiencing a major decline in lasting marriages. From celebrities and billionaires to newlyweds and even experienced couples, it seems that there is no end to the rising divorce rate. With all these divorces in mind, the question on everyone's lips is, "What's the problem in all these marriages?"

Men have been conditioned to believe that all they need to do is reach a place of financial security, and once they're able to provide that security to a woman, there will be no issues—plain and simple. But when we consider highly-publicized divorces, such as that of Bill and Melinda Gates, it becomes clear that money isn't the factor.

Don't get me wrong—it's in a man's nature to be a provider, especially for those whom he loves. As a matter of fact, it is this very love that propels him to generate wealth so that his family feels safe and protected. As such, we can agree that in most cases, love isn't actually what's lacking in most marriages, because men prove their love for their wives through their actions. But this brings us back to what God asked of wives. With the husband's love accounted for in our modern world, what about the wife's respect?

Contrary to popular belief, love is not the only requirement that ensures a lasting and healthy marriage or romantic relationship. The truth is that men and women are wired differently, and therefore have different ways of expressing their love for each other. Men, traditionally, are known to show their love in very practical ways, such as being their wives' protection, physically and emotionally. And as we just covered, men also show their love by providing financial stability, comfort, and affection.

In turn, women naturally reciprocate by showing respect to their husbands for the effort they are making to build the life they desire. In essence, respecting her husband is a woman's way of showing appreciation for his hard work. This proves that love and respect have a unique effect on both parties, and that's because there is a tangible difference between the two.

You may have noticed a high volume of self-help books coming out these days that are targeted at wives, offering them solutions to improving their marriages. If you've ever cracked one open, isn't it strange how most seem to focus on ways that they should love their spouse better? Even when the topic of respect is addressed, the advice is usually geared toward love. But as I mentioned, a woman's expression of love toward her husband is not the correct antidote to remedy a strained relationship. Unfortunately, though, not enough wives today seem to know this. Even within the Christian faith, there seems to be a greater emphasis placed on wives loving their husbands instead of respecting them.

To prove the great misunderstanding that exists when defining love and respect in the faith-based community, let me tell you a little story: The daughter of a prominent evangelical figure was giving advice to women on ways they can show respect to their husbands. She said that wives should be grateful for their husbands' efforts by lauding them with verbal affirmations. These affirmations could be for the little things they do, like taking out the trash or helping out with the children.

She advised these women to express their gratitude by telling their spouses how much they appreciate them helping out around the house or playing with the kids to give her a break. But what the daughter of this Christian leader failed to understand is that words of affirmation are not an act of respect—rather, they are just another method of expressing love. Now, is expressing love to your husband in a variety of ways a bad thing? Not at all. As a matter of fact, I'll encourage you to read up on the five love languages so that you and your husband can both express your love to each other in the most fulfilling ways possible.

Nonetheless, we're back to the premise of this very book: Loving your husband isn't the same as respecting him. No matter what methods you employ to express love to your husband, they will never satisfy his need to be respected. Not only that, but you won't be fulfilling your obligation as a wife before God to respect your husband. If you desire to love and serve God, part of doing that as a wife is—once more—a requirement to respect your husband. But with how blurred the lines have become between love and respect in so many marriages, you're going to need some clear guidance to effectively respect your husband, and, furthermore, enjoy a long-lasting and more harmonious marriage. And that, of course, is where I step in.

Make no mistakes, this book is not going to be filled with generic wordplay about "spicing up" your relationship through love, passion, lust, excitement, or seduction techniques. Oftentimes, the answers to our marital problems are simple, and that's why the content you'll be engaging with here is specifically about how to respect your husband.

Keep in mind that this isn't meant to be a rigid manual for you to follow. After all, my intention is for you to cultivate a better relationship with your husband—nothing more. And it also doesn't discount the fact that there are indeed other ways to improve your relationship, such as the methods of lust, passion, and love I mentioned earlier. But, simply put, that's not what we're covering here.

Before we get started, I just want to say that while this book is meant to target women in particular, in no way is it meant to denigrate or paint you or any other women in a negative light. I intended to write this book from a purely positive and practical standpoint. All I really want is to provide you with actionable steps that you can employ in your relationship. As such, what you won't find is a list of bad behaviors and traits that you should discontinue, like "Stop nagging your husband" or "Stop criticizing everything about your husband."

Instead, I'm going to be providing you with a list of good behaviors that you can adopt. With great effort taken in understanding the issues of our present generation, I have also tried to fashion the tips in this book to fit into the modern cultural context so that they may apply better to you. This was done with the mindfulness that much of our culture has become so adulterated that it actively disrespects men, and husbands in particular. So, undoubtedly, many of the suggestions will be countercultural in nature. Nevertheless, if applied correctly and with the right attitude, I wholeheartedly believe the information in this book will change your relationship with your husband for the better. It will seem almost miraculous, in fact.

Chapter 1:
Allow Him to Parent His Children Without Your Intervention

Let Dad Do His Thing

When God designed Eve, he purposefully incorporated an extra dose of maternal instinct in her. From the shape of her physique and the specified functions of her body parts to the more gentle, nurturing energy she exuded, Eve—and all women to come after her—was made with a more affectionate, motherly nature than Adam.

Now, although the first word spoken by most babies is "Dada," it's no wonder why they never fail to reach for their mothers in times of distress. It's because babies can instinctively tell the difference in energy between the mother and the father. But where mothers are strong in the nurturing aspect, fathers are seen early on as a pillar of strength and discipline.

As a result of this innate nurturing disposition, a wife may tend to feel like she has a better understanding when it comes to raising children than her husband. This, then, may lead to an ever-present temptation to interfere in the parenting style of their husband, but it doesn't do justice to the children. Why? Because a wife's failure to allow her husband to fulfill his fatherly role not only communicates a lack of respect for their children but also demonstrates that this wife lacks faith in her husband's competence to perform his duties.

To further understand how a wife's interference in her husband's parenting style shows a lack of respect, let's dive a bit deeper into the different approaches to parenting between men and women. We'll find that, while men focus on security in a particular aspect of life (like resources, habitation, and other forms of physical protection), women also focus on security, but with a different approach.

Regardless of the narrative that modern society tries to push, men and women are designed completely differently—there's no getting around this. From the way they think and process information, down to their unique style of parenting, this is a vital fact that warrants appreciation. According to Connolly Counseling Center, women are much better at security in regard to organization and being more lateral, or "multi-object focused." This is the reason why it's often heard that women are better at multitasking, especially when it comes to simultaneously thinking of various different tasks that need to be accomplished (Connolly Counseling Center, 2017).

If you're a woman reading this, you likely understand exactly what I'm saying here. Let's say, for example, that you're preparing for a family trip with your husband and children. With all your essentials packed, your husband is thinking of the task at hand, which is to hop in the vehicle and start driving toward the destination. But as a woman, with your need to feel secure, you will probably be thinking of a myriad of different things, such as whether the house lights will be set on timers while you're away, whether the water has been turned off, and if enough snacks and juices were packed for the kids. In short, women won't truly be at peace until no stone has been left unturned.

Now, another major difference in the hard wiring of men and women results in the opposing ways each gender views the world. These differences can be mutually beneficial when working in sync with one another, so it's fundamental to understand the unique approach each one has to life, and subsequently, to parenting.

Men are generally more task-focused than women, which is where the "one-track mind" thinking is generated. This affects your husband's psychological and emotional state in such a way that when you express your feelings or emotions to him, he may be at a disadvantage. And that's because, as a natural problem-solver, he's thinking of ways to find a solution. As such, his first response might be, "How can I solve this problem?", when in contrast, your only desire is for your emotions to be validated and understood.

Like women, children may also share this need to be heard and understood without necessarily wanting advice. On that note, it's pivotal that when a father listens to his wife and children, he listens with intention to their feelings without being hasty to provide answers or solutions. After listening intently to empathize, assuring you that he understands your feelings (or those of your children), only then should it be possible for him to perform his manly duties by providing solutions and advice.

Differences in Parenting Styles Between Men and Women

But it's also important to know that your husband's methods of solving problems and offering advice, especially to the children, may come across as unloving or harsh at times. Indeed, he may appear to be too hard on the children or push them to their limits. However, this is simply how he intrinsically expresses his love to his children—through discipline, decisiveness, and encouraging them in his own way.

As a wife and mother who is more nurturing and coddling with your approach to children, you may not understand his method of parenting, and this may prompt you to want him to praise your kids' efforts instead of pushing them to do better. But this is where you must restrain the urge to intervene in your husband's more masculine approach to parenting. Why? Because it's a needed part of your children's development.

It's important to understand that this seemingly unemotional demand for excellence from your husband is nothing more than his decision-making ability on display, which is a quality of leadership. In fact, this superior leadership quality in most men causes them to focus on "getting things done" and provoking progress in the areas where they see potential. So, his swift decision-making process, while allowing him to think on his feet and make swift rational decisions, can also cause him to be less emotionally connected.

This is why when he decides that his children are not performing to their fullest potential and chooses to push them, it may come across as insensitive. Furthermore, keep in mind that as a man, your husband has had a different life experience than you, and understands how unforgiving and cruel the world can be. This results in him trying to mold his children to be strong and capable. To put it plainly, he's preparing the kids for the journey of life that awaits them!

Ultimately, your husband understands that his role as protector and provider requires a certain type of character. This is why he has been bestowed with the ability to make tough decisions quickly, accurately, and with little emotion to cloud his judgment.

You may also find that your husband has little tolerance for disobedience or laziness when it comes to raising his children. That's because men have been wired to expect that whenever they make a request for something to be done, it should be done promptly and without question. If you witness this particular behavior in your husband, keep in mind that this is his standard because, for those he is protecting, he knows that giving directives and being clearly understood can be a matter of life and death in certain situations.

In sharp contrast to this, of course, is your softer and more nurturing qualities, and so you may perceive his decisiveness and expectation for obedience as inconsiderate qualities. So, if you notice that your spouse is less tolerant with the children when he asks them to complete a task at home, which they fail to do properly, try to understand that it's coming from a place of genuine masculinity. As such, all that's needed from you is to trust that he knows exactly what he's doing, even though you may approach the situation in a completely different way.

By trusting him to perform his manly duties even when you don't fully understand his methods, you're showing a great deal of respect for his capability to lead as the head of your home.

Differences in Approach to Watching Over the Children

This brings me to my next point, which is the difference in the way men and women mind, or pay attention to, their children. Beginning with women, as I touched on earlier, just as men are skilled at swift decision-making, women are skilled at multitasking. This is because they operate from a different emotional and psychological perspective when it comes to ensuring safety and security.

As a result, the multitasking trait in a woman may lead the children—and even her husband at times—to feel like she is not listening. Because her mind is simultaneously dealing with so many different aspects of life, her lack of eye contact may give off the impression that she is not focusing intently on what is being communicated. But, as I'm sure you know yourself, this appearance is only due to the fact that women are constantly engrossed in activities like ironing clothes, preparing dinner, or doing taxes. In reality, she is still listening to what is happening around her.

Now, children typically require some form of eye contact in order to feel like they are being heard by their parents, of course. As such, you may have to make time for brief eye contact. Failing that, you can always opt for employing some empathetic listening, or repeat what they just said back to them.

On the other hand, a man is often one-dimensional, and would rather commit all his focus to the task at hand without interruption. And so you may find that when your husband takes over the parenting role, the children may feel a tad imprisoned in his care. Indeed, he may sternly insist that they sit still and remain quiet until his task is complete or until he returns. His need to oversee the children constantly is contrary to the way his wife operates, because her multitasking capability enables her to have a sense of their presence, even if they are out of her line of sight.

Understanding That Your Husband's Parenting Style Differs From Yours

Make no mistake, God truly made men and women different in a variety of ways, with a blend of strengths and weaknesses that complement each other. The complementary nature of men and women is meant to be manifested in both their relationship with each other and their relationship with their children.

Each relationship dynamic is unique in its style, but the delicate dance of opposing genders is even more important in parenting because it ultimately shapes the core values and principles of an infant as they grow into an adult. In particular, the way they form and maintain relationships, deal with conflict resolution, and manage their own emotions are all dependent on how they respond to the parenting styles of both the mother and the father.

Of course, no two partnerships are going to be the same, but it's good to have the polar opposites of masculine and feminine at work because it helps to mold the child into a well-rounded individual. Under these dual influences, they're able to differentiate between the primary responsibilities assigned to the roles of each parent, providing them with an example of caretaking values.

Moving along, here are some of the core differences between men and women in terms of parenting, and why those differences matter to the upbringing of the child.

Dads Focus on the Big Picture, Moms Focus on the Details

Dr. Meg Meeker, the author of *Strong Fathers, Strong Daughters*, had this to say about the pivotal roles fathers occupy in the lives of their children, and how it targets a specifically different area when it comes to a child's character development: "Dads approach parenting with different priorities than we mothers do. They tend to care less about dress, eating habits, and other details. Instead, dads tend to want to play with kids more and challenge them more, and this can help kids gain confidence" (Bush, 2016).

With the traditional roles of mothers and fathers being blurred in our modern society, this may not always reflect properly in every household. However, it does highlight the stereotypical strengths of men and women both in personal and professional settings. Furthermore, this can be supported in how we have thus far characterized women and men, and their respective multitasking and leadership capabilities.

These "stereotypical" roles, when performed correctly, bring a much-needed balance to the home, and help in building sound character and morale in children. This is why, oftentimes, you find that mothers, who have stronger organizational skills, tend to be more focused on everyday details, like creating schedules and assigning chores. In contrast, dads are playing the roles of both friend and authoritarian, which develops both the character and confidence of the child.

The Dynamics of Competition vs Fairness

Here, we have another stereotypical aspect of the nature of masculine and feminine energy at play in parenting roles. Speaking of play, the way in which fathers and mothers engage in playful activities with their children is a great way of showcasing the values held by each gender.

When fathers are engaged in play, they tend to emphasize the spirit of competition, while mothers exhibit equity and fairness. These are both necessary when it comes to instilling essential values and personality traits that, if not equally contributed, can lead to a faulty foundation and an uncertain future for the child.

However, it's important to note that the experiences of both the man and woman determine the way in which they parent their children. For example, if the father was taught to be competitive and a risk-taker, then by default, he teaches his children to embody these same traits, which affects the way they interact with the world and handle life's obstacles.

Women, on the other hand, are taught self-preservation and to treat others with equity, which are also skills that will be passed on to their children as valuable wisdom to be used for safely navigating life. When combined, these two life perspectives work together to bring about a balanced individual who learns to be fair while having a competitive edge, as these are required attributes to get ahead in the world.

The Dichotomy of Nurture vs Discipline

Now, while both mother and father are able to administer strict discipline to their children, there's something about a father's presence that does so naturally—almost effortlessly, in fact. That's because, as the mother, your natural function is that of a nurturer. Being that mothers are more cautious, protective, and focused on safety and fairness when it comes to the children, the way you enforce discipline may come across as being "too soft" in the eyes of your husband. It's at this point that a man's presence exudes that of "the disciplinarian," bringing about much-needed law and order in the family unit.

Dad's fun, interactive, yet disciplinarian nature is established in the younger years of the children's lives, but it becomes more apparent as they become teenagers. As with most children, the teenage years are often accompanied by a degree of defiance and rebellion toward authority. Even as adults today, we can recall that phase of life when we thought we were untouchable, were above parental guidance and admonition, and were ready to grab the world by its proverbial horns.

When conflict arises during this time, which it most likely will, Mom may be more inclined to be the peacemaker and try to accommodate the children as much as possible. On the other hand, Dad approaches conflict as an opportunity for a lesson to be taught as opposed to trying to avoid disagreements.

Here is where the man needs to be respected for the way in which he deals with child-parent conflict. You see, getting in the way of what you perceive as "tough love" could actually be robbing your child of valuable life lessons that would serve them in the long run. Men, who are more rational in their thinking, understand the coldness of the world, and to survive in it requires a certain level of grit and backbone. He understands that being too lenient and agreeable with the children sets them up for failure as adults when they leave the comfort of the family home.

So, instead of giving in to the urge to intervene and soften the impact of the tough lessons they're being taught by their father, the mother should praise the efforts of her husband to mold strong and dependable individuals.

Once again, in our modern society, it's not uncommon for the roles to get reversed, where Dad takes a more hands-on approach to the responsibilities that are traditionally reserved for Mom. This may include things like the role of caretaker, while she leads the way as the disciplinarian. However, if you and your spouse decide to perform your individual roles, the one thing you need to ensure is that you provide the balance between support and discipline so that your children can positively benefit from it.

Emotionally Attached vs Emotionally Detached

It's often been said that women are emotional creatures, and that is seen in the deeper emotional attachment they tend to share with their loved ones, especially those they nurture, like, obviously, their spouse and children. Now, that isn't to say that fathers love their children any less than mothers—ideally, they should both love their children equally. But undoubtedly, a mother's emotional attachment seems to be more evident based on the expectations that are placed on her.

Just take the prevalent issue of single-parent households that we see so much of today. While there may be the exception of single-father households, we generally find that after a divorce or failed relationship, the mother takes full responsibility for caring for the children. Fathers are not held to such high expectations when it comes to emotional attachment with their children because they are relegated to a supportive role.

Even within functioning, healthy households where the mother and father understand their roles and are on one accord, the mother still displays a greater level of emotional attachment to her children. In comparison, a man tends to detach much more easily because he understands that his role as a masculine figure is to provide and protect. He needs to "go on the hunt," so to speak, to ensure that his family is secure financially, physically, emotionally, and socially.

During those times he is at home, he lends support to his wife by playing with the children, teaching them valuable lessons, and encouraging the dynamics of competition and discipline that we discussed earlier. But as a mother, how are you affected by the high expectations of emotional attachment with your children? If you're a stay-at-home mom, this can lead to feelings of being overly emotional and overworked. And if you're a working mom, your maternal attachment may cause you to feel guilty for not being at home, especially during the child's infancy stages.

Another noticeable difference between the emotional and detachment styles of women and men is found in the way they communicate, both as a couple and with their children. Because of a man's solution-oriented mind, his words can be few and to the point. Women, on the other hand, tend to be more investigative, which is again a reflection of emotional investment.

This doesn't mean that Dad is any less invested in the lives of their children than Mom is, but it speaks to the fact that a parent's role in the family can have an impact on their ability to detach easily.

In our modern age of technology, there are some fathers who work from home while their wives work in a corporate job setting. This, of course, depends heavily on the career/occupation of each parent. Nevertheless, because of the dichotomy in the way men and women are wired, women will more often than not have a stronger emotional attachment to the kids. Meanwhile, a man—if he is a traditional man—will be a pillar of support to his wife, offering her an emotional break when he is around the children.

Showing Respect and Trust

When it comes down to it, there are many ways you can start showing respect to your husband. But, in many cases, the problem is not figuring out what ways you can start to show respect, but rather discerning the patterns of behavior that communicate a lack of respect. By knowing what *not* to do, you'll be avoiding the potential for disrespect altogether.

We'll get into some of the other ways you can begin to show respect to your husband as it pertains to your marital bond, but let's start with allowing him to perform his parental duties. There's nothing that makes a man feel more undervalued and undermined than a wife who doesn't trust him to step into his masculine role and take leadership, especially as a parent. With that in mind, here are a series of steps worth taking note of.

1. **Acknowledge his parental decisions.**

As a woman who is more compassionate and tolerant with her children, you may not always understand or agree with your husband's parenting methods. But as long as he is not causing extreme harm or danger to your children, you'll need to take a step back and allow him to fulfill his role as the source of masculine parental energy in the household.

If he appears to be stricter with the children when it comes to things like managing playtime and study time or cutting back on how much time is spent on electronics, he's only bringing a sense of order, balance, and accountability to the kids. By questioning his decisions in front of them, you're not only showing a lack of respect for his authority, but you're also inviting the children to lose respect for him as well.

To sum up, by questioning his decisions, you are inadvertently stating that he isn't good at parenting, which diminishes his role as leader of the family, bringing in chaos, confusion, and rebellion.

2. Support his ideas.

Supporting your husband's ideas goes hand in hand with supporting his decisions, and it's an excellent way to demonstrate your respect for him. These ideas can be business-related or personal, but when he expresses them to you, it is with the intention of gaining your support. So, whether it's an idea to incorporate physical exercise into the children's daily routine, or he's sharing a business idea that he wants you to embark on with him—all he's asking for is your support.

Similarly, by supporting his ideas—especially when it pertains to family—you're communicating to the children that you trust his guidance and you're willing to follow his initiative. When your support for your husband is strong, there will be no room for divisiveness among the children because you are presenting a united front.

3. Resist criticisms.

As much as the urge may be there to nitpick at every area that you think your husband could improve in, it's not the best way to show that you respect his need for peace. So, after your husband returns home from a long day at work where he's been figuratively slaying giants and fighting temptations, the last thing he wants to come home to is another battle with your mouth.

Constantly complaining and criticizing about every small detail can be extremely draining, both for you and your husband. When he's expending energy to maintain your basic needs, and presumably even some of your wants, and he's being further drained by your incessant complaints, you're discouraging and demotivating him from putting in any extra effort into the marriage.

Indeed, when his endeavors are met with a lack of gratitude, it may lead him to pull away emotionally and shut down in an attempt to retreat to a place of peace. This is not the kind of atmosphere you want to create in your marriage, because, after all, you are supposed to produce an environment of peace—especially in the home.

So, instead of complaining about minor inconsistencies, try altering your perspective and finding things to be grateful for that your husband does, even if these things are seemingly insignificant. And if you've learned these behaviors by surrounding yourself with a circle of married friends who enjoy gossiping and complaining about their husbands, it would be in your best interest to start weeding out the Negative Nancys around you.

Remember that misery loves company, and even though your marriage seems to be problem-free now, hanging around people who only speak negatively about their spouses may easily influence you to start looking for the worst in your partner. And without a doubt, that's the fastest and easiest way to make anyone feel underappreciated. As 1 Corinthians 15:33 states, "Be not deceived: evil communications corrupt good manners" (King James Bible Online, 1611).

4. Avoid making comparisons.

According to an article from Focus On the Family, it's never wise to compare your husband to other men of faith, or even the husbands of your friends (Arbuckle, 2020). In fact, it's important to realize that your husband is not a perfect leader, as no one on Earth is perfect. What you need to do, then, is balance respect for your husband with the reality that he is not a perfect leader.

By keeping his imperfections in mind, you'll be reminded that he is a work in progress, which will inspire you to shift your perspective from comparing his inefficiencies to others to recognizing and appreciating his unique strengths and skills. Don't forget: Your husband is an original handiwork of God who has equipped him with all the qualities needed to fulfill his purpose on Earth, which includes caring for his family. Therefore, as his wife, you should be less concerned with comparing his style of leadership with that of your friends' husbands.

5. Choose to respect your husband.

It's been said that a well-cooked meal is the key to a man's heart, but that couldn't be further from the truth. Respect is not only the key to a man's heart but also to his confidence. As his wife, you should never underestimate the immense impact respect has on him, because he values it coming from you more than anyone else in the world. And by trusting him to lead your family in spite of his imperfections without succumbing to your desire to intervene, you're sending a message of absolute respect.

Going back to the connection between respect and confidence, by choosing to respect your husband, you're also building his confidence, which directly affects the way he shows up in every other area of life. So, by respecting your husband, you're helping to make him a better man and leader not just for your household, but for the community at large.

Letting Your Husband Lead Without the Need to Intervene

Now, there are many women who hate to admit it (while others are brutally honest), but they love a man who can take charge. It's the reason why men are expected to embody the more dominant role they often do and take the lead in romantic relationships. Not to mention being the leader within the family.

But many times, because of your difference in opinion and perspective, you may be led to think that your husband is not performing his leadership duties optimally, which can cause you to want to intervene. And while that might seem like the helpful and even natural thing to do, it's actually counterproductive. How could that be? Well, it's ultimately because, as we now know, it comes across as a subtle sign of disrespect.

The husband is actually required by God to take the leadership role in a way that exhibits a balance between strong leadership and compassionate tenderness. This is a picture of how Christ loves the Church, as Ephesians 5:25 states, "Husbands, love your wives, even as Christ also loved the church, and gave himself for it" (King James Bible Online, 1611b).

As his wife, if you desire for yourself and your family to be led correctly by your husband, you'll need to encourage him to embrace his leadership role. As a matter of fact, doing this will eliminate many marital problems (if there are any, to begin with) because the relationship will be in its rightful, godly order—the man loving his wife, and the wife respecting her husband.

Taken from Mrs. Midwest, here are a few biblical prescriptions that can be utilized that will allow your husband to lead without intervening (Cait, 2020). This next batch of tips you can think of as a cheat code to strengthen your marital bond by fully embracing your role as your spouse's helpmeet, all the while encouraging him to step fully into his leadership position.

1. **Listen with intent.**

While there is truth behind the notion that women tend to be better communicators than men, that doesn't mean you should dismiss your husband's thoughts and ideas when he decides to share them. The fact that he may find it more difficult to share his thoughts and ideas with you, and still makes an effort to express them, should be all the more reason why you should respect him for doing so.

Remember that he greatly values your time and attention when listening to him. Today's society is quick to cancel men for simply sharing ideas or expressing perspectives that are out of the ordinary or that go against what is deemed politically correct. So, when he chooses to communicate those thoughts and feelings, even if they're unpopular, practice active listening by nodding and looking him in the eye when he speaks.

That means setting aside your phone and any other distractions you'll find to tune out his suggestions, especially if he's saying something you don't agree with or think you already know about. This also acts as another great show of respect and lets him know that you're engaged in what he's saying.

This brings me to the next point, which is learning to listen when you are in a debate or heated discussion. Did you know that many times, people think they are arguing or debating with someone when, in actuality, they have already dismissed the perspective of the other? And therefore, they can't actually appreciate a word they say!

Indeed, arguments generally escalate because one or both persons have already mentally blocked out what the other is saying. But during those moments when you are having a tough discussion with your husband, instead of assuming you already know why he's thinking from a certain perspective, try to listen intently to the words coming out of his mouth. That way, your debates may turn into opportunities for learning and growth instead of a stubborn back-and-forth.

Now, you may be surprised to learn that by resisting the urge to intervene with your own ideas when it comes to solving an issue and truly listening, you could be avoiding unnecessary frustration. But it's true! Again, if you want your husband to be in a place of leadership, you have to be willing to let him lead. And you can do that by withholding your tongue and allowing him to present his thoughts and ideas as practical solution. By forfeiting your need to always be right and listening to his arguments, you're communicating that you respect him and are comfortable with him taking the lead.

2. Take a back seat: Allow him to be the boss.

Just like with resisting the need to intervene, there is a lot of value in having the willingness to pull back the reins of your usual propensity to take charge, whether voluntarily or involuntarily. When you do, you're simply giving your husband space to operate in the leadership role that he's meant to personify.

Does this mean that you should be passive, less engaged, or uninvolved? Not in the least. Rather, you're making a conscious decision to allow your husband to step up and exercise his authority in making decisions for your family. Most women say they feel as though they're "mothering" their husband when in reality they're complaining about his lack of initiative in decision-making. This generally stems from their own desire to be in charge, which interferes with their husband's life and encroaches on his manhood. In other words, how can he be the masculine leader you desire him to be if you always try to dictate the narrative of every situation?

And keep in mind that this applies in other situations too, not just when making life-changing decisions. You could start by giving him room to make smaller decisions in everyday life, which is exactly what you should want in a masculine leader. This could take the shape of letting him choose an alternative route home from work or allowing him to decide how he would like to spend his leisure time.

The thing is, a man feels most in his masculine energy when he feels useful to those around him. So, when it comes to DIY jobs around the home that he can fix, respect him by allowing him to take charge in doing those things without feeling the need to hover over his every decision.

Now, you may be apprehensive about this at first because you think if he takes on more responsibility, it will lead to chaos in the household. But if your complaint is that you feel like you're "mothering" him, then this is the way in which he will grow. Men grow through trial and error, after all, and if you want your husband to be more of a leader, you first need to present him with more opportunities for growth.

It's counterintuitive to assume a leadership role in your marriage by trying to dictate every aspect of your marriage, and then turn around and complain that your husband isn't taking charge and being a leader. Maybe when he attempts to do that, he's met with your combative and uncooperative spirit, which then makes him want to take a step back in order to keep the peace.

This is how many marriages fall apart—there are two people simultaneously trying to wear the leadership hat in the relationship. In healthy marriages, the masculine partner assumes his role as the more dominant force and leads accordingly, while the woman steps into her feminine nature, and allows the man to lead.

3. Allow him to fail.

Bridging off of the last point about taking a back seat, this "allowance" is crucial. Think of it this way: Giving your husband space to be the boss also means having the grace to allow him to fail at times. Even the most capable of leaders fall short at times. And if you're having a hard time believing that, just consider yourself: How many mistakes do *you* make on a daily basis?

The main reason why women are filled with trepidation when it comes to allowing their husbands to take the reins, much less make mistakes, is because there is a stereotypical view of men in our culture that they are just big kids; *man-childs*. Therefore, women believe that they can't be trusted with too much responsibility.

Some women even believe that without their intervention, the entire house would go up in smoke. Such narratives are also propagated by mass media and the entertainment industry, portraying mothers and heroines who step in and save a chaotic household from an incompetent father. But don't let these things fool you: Respect is shown by trusting your husband to lead when the opportunity arises, and also not holding it against him whenever mistakes are made. You don't want to create an environment where respect is only shown when he succeeds— it's just as important for him to feel respect when he fails. This builds trust, intimacy, and understanding between the two of you.

If you've been critical in the past whenever he has failed, try showing some grace and understanding, as this will secure his confidence. Remember that none of us is perfect, and we all fail. So, if you're expecting perfection in leadership, especially from a man who has not been given many opportunities by his wife to display leadership, then it's time to change your perspective.

To avoid disappointment, you should actually embark on this journey with the expectation that your husband *will* fail at times. By taking this approach, you won't resort to your default reactions of being overly critical and condescending. Instead, plan a healthier response ahead of time for when he does make a mistake.

Proverbs 18:21 says, "Death and life are in the power of the tongue: and they that love it shall eat the fruit thereof" (King James Bible Online, 1611c). Use this scripture verse as a reminder to *speak life* to your husband even in times of failure. By being graceful, understanding, and forgiving of his hiccups, you'll help him feel confident enough to take on future leadership opportunities.

4. Let him have the last word.

Part of resisting the urge to intervene is allowing your husband to have the final word in a conversation or when making a decision. If mulling over two options, let him choose what he likes best without reservation. Making a decision about where to go out for dinner? Go willingly with his selection—no complaints! What sense does it make to agree with his decision and then look for every reason to fuss about why you don't like the cuisine? That's almost the same as saying you forgive someone for an offense but then bringing it up in conversation every chance you get.

Letting him have the final say and happily going along with his decision is a highly effective way of letting him be the leader. Most modern households employ the formula "happy wife, happy life," which essentially gives the power to the wife, allowing her to have the final say. But, as per the results shown by the recent divorce rate, that formula has proven to be ineffective.

The point is, resisting the need to argue your point until you have the final say will make your husband feel loved and respected. Not only that, but you'll also feel a deeper attraction to him because you will feel less compelled to make the final decision, as you begin to trust his judgment more and more.

Now, going back to the aspect of added responsibility, your husband will come to realize the weight he has to bear when it comes to having the last word. In particular, he will understand that having the final word when making a decision in any situation, big or small, will affect both of you as well as your children.

And so, when you contain your need to intervene in his decision-making process, you're helping him to fulfill his God-given right as leader, protector, and provider. This will also, in turn, cause you to embrace your feminine nature, leaving you both feeling happier and more satisfied in the marriage and as a family unit.

Alright—now that you have a clearer understanding of how to respect your husband by way of leading effectively as a parent and a partner, it's time to move on to Chapter 2, where we will address another common trait of disrespect: speaking well of your husband, both in his presence and with others.

Failure to speak positively about your partner, especially when among family and friends, not only conveys your disrespect for him in the relationship but also invites others to disrespect him as well. Let's find out how the simple act of choosing to *speak life* to your husband in his absence is a reflection of your loyalty, support, and most of all, your respect for him.

Chapter 2:
Speak Well of Him With Others

Protect His Reputation

It must be understood that marriage unions are not for the faint of heart, and they're definitely not for those without self-control. They require a great deal of effort from both the man and the woman, who must commit to fighting for peace, understanding, unity, and mutual respect.

But, with our focus being on women, we must turn our attention next to a common habit: conversing with female friends and family. Of course, there's nothing wrong inherently with this practice, but nonetheless, this is the prime place to practice the next lesson: speaking well of your husband. As a wife, you represent your husband based on how you show up in the world, and this includes the way you speak about him to others.

Even if the two of you are going through a momentary rough patch, if the comments you make about him and the information you divulge to others focus mostly on the negative aspects of the relationship, it's likely not going to end well. And, God forbid, if this rough patch does end in divorce, it would be largely due to the atmosphere surrounding the marriage that your words helped to create outside of the home.

This brings us back to the scripture I mentioned in the previous chapter—"Death and life are in the power of the tongue: and they that love it shall eat the fruit thereof." The application of this scripture is fitting in various areas of life, including marriage. Essentially, Proverbs 18:21 is telling us that we have the power, through our words, to create the life we want professionally and personally.

Again, let's say you and your husband are going through a marriage trial, and instead of loving and supporting him by speaking of his best qualities, you choose to betray the trust of your union by speaking ill of him. When you do this, even if it seems minor, you're doing yourself a huge disservice—plain and simple. There's no getting around it: Couples who choose to work through their marital issues together and present one another as upright and committed will find success.

Don't mistake this with keeping up a facade in your marriage. Indeed, resisting the urge to speak negatively about your husband in public settings isn't the same as pretending there aren't flaws within your marriage that need to be fixed. However, it's an entirely different dynamic when you and your husband have agreed to actively work on your marital problems together while deciding not to air out your dirty laundry to friends and family.

When handling your marital problems, privacy is the best policy. But in the event that you're asked about your husband by a friend, speaking well of him in their presence is a testament to your character and shows that you have his best interest at heart. And this, conveniently, brings us to our next point: how your words about your spouse reflect right back on you.

Speaking Well of Your Husband Is a Positive Reflection on You

Your tongue is one of the smallest muscles in the human anatomy, and yet it's one of the most powerful. How is that, you ask? Well, you may be familiar with the old proverb that goes, "When you point a finger, there are three fingers pointing back at you." Basically, what this means is that when you take the time to point out the flaws in others, you can expect that in return, many more fingers will be pointing out the flaws in you.

So, when you point out the flaws and mistakes of someone close to you, like your husband, you're essentially bringing your own character into question as well as setting yourself up to be criticized by others. And it's for this very reason that, according to professional couples counselor Mike Dawson and his wife Susan, you should strive to keep your daily conversations about your husband as positive as possible (Dawson, 2017). By doing so, you're also shedding a positive light on yourself.

The idea of benefiting from talking well of others is also scientifically proven. When you choose to speak positively about others, you're partaking in a phenomenon known as "spontaneous trait transference," which occurs when communicators are perceived as taking on the same traits and qualities they describe in others.

So, the next time you're hanging out with your girlfriends and they all start spilling the tea on their marriage lives, consider what you're going to say when all the eyes fall on you. When they do, be sure to say something like, "My husband is so wise, caring, and patient with me. And he's always thinking of creative ways to show me how much he appreciates me."

Even though your friends may not have experienced those traits in your husband in the same way you have, by describing him in such a positive light, you're also making those traits more visible in yourself.

Now, on a human psychological level, the characteristics spoken about when describing others automatically become associated with the person speaking—you, in this case. This also enables you to more easily influence specific trait implications, which tend to persist over time.

Beyond science, God has also designed us to honor and model the traits and characteristics we admire in others, similar to the way in which we praise and seek to exemplify the admirable qualities of Christ (something believers are actually called to do, after all). And while this doesn't imply that you should worship your husband, it does highlight the fact that when you choose to speak highly of him, you also begin to adopt them as your own.

Now, in contrast, the spontaneous trait transference also applies when you choose to underscore the lesser qualities of your spouse. In fact, those negative characteristics become associated with you, and the associations persist over time as well. There was certainly much wisdom in what many of us were taught as children—"If you have nothing nice to say, don't say anything at all."

If speaking negatively about your husband is a bad habit that has been encouraged by your friends or family members, you can dare to be different by associating yourself with your husband's good character qualities. Furthermore, you can limit the amount of time you spend with those particular friends and family members, because as we discussed in Chapter 1, 1 Corinthians 15:33 still rings true: "Be not deceived: evil communications corrupt good manners" (King James Bible Online, 1611).

How Does Speaking Well of Your Husband Better Your Marriage?

I'm sure we can all agree that infidelity is the ultimate betrayal of one's trust in a committed marriage. However, the decision for one partner to break the trust in a relationship doesn't happen overnight, and in fact, is often preceded by a loss of respect. And so, if you find yourself consistently devaluing your spouse both privately and publicly (especially publicly), then you're breaking the fundamental pillars of trust and respect.

In the absence of trust and respect, a good relationship cannot exist—it's a simple truth. And with that in mind, by expressing genuine appreciation for your spouse (especially in the presence of others), you're helping to foster an atmosphere of mutual honor and respect.

Speaking Well of Your Spouse Encourages Others

When you speak well of your husband in front of others, you are not only practicing respecting him, but you are gaining the respect of others. They get to witness your respect for him outside of his presence, and as such, they will respect that you are not two-faced. Again, this is a testament to your character and the unfailing loyalty that you and your husband share together.

Obviously, the same can be reversed when you're constantly speaking negatively about your husband with others. Even though those listening to you may be open to empathizing and comforting you, it's natural for them to wonder if you would also verbally bash them behind their backs as you've done with your spouse.

If the person you're confiding in is a friend, family member, or coworker, their level of trust for you may also be diminishing as they notice your betrayal of someone who is close to you. That being said, there is good news here: When you decide to sing the praises of your husband and highlight the better parts of your relationship, by default, you're encouraging other couples to focus on the positive aspects of their own marriage relationships.

Reaping From the Seeds You Sow

When you pay attention to—and *reinforce*—the traits and characteristics that you admire most about your spouse, you're essentially getting more of what you admire out of him. On that note, when you speak about your husband with someone else, think of your words as seeds that are being planted. If those seeds reflect praiseworthy reports about characteristics you admire in him, then you'll be promoting those characteristics, and in turn, getting more of them in your marriage.

For example, when you're with a friend, you could say something akin to this: "I really love it when Chris sets aside time to help with the children's homework. He's so patient with them and breaks down complex topics in a way that's easy to understand. The children love how he teaches them, and I'm certainly not gifted when it comes to simplifying complex topics."

By declaring this, you're confirming that not only does Chris enjoy helping his children succeed in their schoolwork, but he also appreciates the admiration he receives for it. Thus, he'll continue helping with their homework willingly because you noticed the positive thing he was doing and expressed appreciation.

The Power of Positive Words

As children, many of us repeated the classic phrase, "Sticks and stones may break my bones, but words shall never hurt me." While the intention behind saying this may have been to block out the harmful words of others and grow a thicker skin, the truth is that the words spoken by others can—and do—have an immense impact on our lives.

As I mentioned earlier, our words have the power to either give life or death, and as such, they can either build someone up or tear them down. The outcome you choose to bring about is solely dependent on the words you use when speaking about someone, whether in their presence or behind their back.

So, remember that, as one of the closest people in his life, your words will directly affect your husband's influence as a leader. And therefore, it's unrealistic of you to expect him to be a healthy, functional leader for you and your family while you're consistently displaying a lack of respect for him in both private and in public through the words you speak.

By avoiding negative and disparaging comments about your husband, you're choosing to build him up into the confident, capable, and competent man he is meant to be, as well as strengthening your marital bond. And with that said, let's now go over some ways to avoid falling into the trap of negative talk, according to ChurchLeaders.com (Doyle, 2019). These are proven, biblical methods that will ensure you always speak well of your husband:

1. Choose words that honor your husband.

Ensure that your words are used to honor and esteem your partner. This applies to both husbands and wives, but for the sake of this book, it's mainly targeted at wives. It's been said that, as women tend to be more socially adept and better communicators than men, their words can be used as a force to generate either tranquility or destruction.

Therefore, women must strive to communicate respectfully with their husbands, since respect, once more, is what men thrive on. Now, the following scripture perfectly conveys what God expects from men in marriage, as well as the manner in which women are meant to treat their husbands:

Ephesians 5:33: "Nevertheless let every one of you in particular so love his wife even as himself; and the wife see that she reverence her husband" (King James Bible Online, 1611b).

2. Discuss before what you're allowed to share.

There are some people who can't help but overshare whenever they get excited in a conversation. If this sounds like you, then it's best to discuss with your husband what details of your personal life are allowed to be shared outside of the marriage. Even though you may be talking with mutual friends, there are some things that your husband may prefer to keep private in this company all the same, or even just for the moment.

Indeed, there could be sensitive information he would rather you keep reserved until a later date. But how would you know what information he wants you to share unless you both discuss it beforehand? That's precisely why you two should openly express to each other what can be said in public settings, if anything at all.

3. Be mindful of your motives.

When it comes to sharing information about your husband, there are two things you should always keep in mind:

- **What is the intent?**

    - Try to be vulnerable enough to ask yourself, "Is the information I'm sharing meant to make me look like the better person?"

    - You could also ask yourself, "Am I sharing this information to paint a negative image of my husband in the eyes of others while trying to hide the flaws in myself?"

- **What is the content**
    - While the details or events you're sharing may be factual, this doesn't mean that sharing them would be in the best interest of your husband.

So, consider this: Will the disclosure of your husband's private information to others bring embarrassment or shame to him? Comments can quickly lead to slander and gossip, which are two things the Bible condemns partaking in. So again, tread lightly when divulging what you are sharing—and how you are sharing it.

In whatever setting you find yourself, whether that be personal, professional, or casual, as a member of the body of Christ, your words should be used to draw others closer to God. And simply put, when you're actively engaging in gossip with your friends or coworkers about your husband, you're not doing this.

The following scripture sums this up excellently:

Ephesians 4:29: "Let no corrupt communication proceed out of your mouth, but that which is good to the use of edifying, that it may minister grace unto the hearers."

Avoiding Negative Comments About Your Spouse for a Stronger Marriage

I can't stress enough that the way you communicate with your husband directly affects the quality of his leadership. According to Michael Hyatt from Full Focus, honorable communication with your spouse begins at home, and communicating effectively at home leads to being effective in the professional world (Hyatt, 2016).

The following list will explore why publicly praising your husband is one of the best investments you can make for your marriage and for your family, as well as for your husband's effective leadership in the outside world:

4. Get more of what you want through affirmation.

As we touched on earlier, it's in our nature as humans to repeat the behavior that caused someone to praise us. Think of the way a child responds when they are praised for good behavior, or for passing a test they studied hard for. As a parent, they greatly value your acknowledgment and approval of their hard work, which inspires them to want to repeat the behavior they've been praised for.

This is the same effect your praise has on your husband when you praise the positive aspects of his character or acknowledge his efforts. It's a powerful way to motivate him to repeat those positive characteristics in order to keep the praise coming! In short, everyone likes to know they're being appreciated for their good qualities.

Although this can be a powerful tool for motivation, this method works in the opposite way as well. The more you complain about your partner's mistakes or poor characteristics, the more of that behavior you'll get. And if you've only been calling out the negative areas of your spouse and seeing no change, then maybe it's time to switch up the game plan.

Instead of honing in on all his negative traits (with no success), try to recognize his good traits and validate them. And, as you now know, by doing that, you'll be reinforcing those positive traits and building an altogether healthier relationship.

5. Your affirmations can affect your attitude.

Going back to Proverbs 18:21, we can agree that our words are powerful enough to not only create the life we want but to also inspire or demoralize another person. As you may know, negative words spoken about someone can begin to affect your attitude toward them.

However, this may not be the case with your husband. The negative things you say about him may actually be helping to form your attitude toward him. In fact, your attitude speaks to the condition of your heart, as Matthew 12:34 says, "O ye generation of vipers, how can ye, being evil, speak good thing? for out of the abundance of the heart, the mouth speaketh" (King James Bible Online, 1611c).

It's quite possible that, if you can correct your words, your attitude may also begin to shift. Your choice to *speak life* is an invitation to either focus on the positive or negative attributes of your husband. And if you are willing to focus on his positive qualities and affirm them with your words, then your attitude toward him will eventually be brought into alignment.

6. Affirmation brings out the best in your marriage.

Your affirmations are a dose of encouragement for your husband, pushing him to continue putting his best foot forward as a man. Truly, your positive and endearing words are powerful and, when used effectively, can strengthen your spouse's best qualities or even bring out qualities that have been dormant.

For example, if your husband is skillful in a certain area, exercises great patience, or is full of compassion, then affirming those qualities in him will only make them stronger. Try remembering that the more you affirm the qualities you want to see, the more likely they will appear.

7. Affirmation repels temptation.

The effects of betrayal in a relationship can sometimes be irreparable. And so, the best way to avoid the possibility of infidelity in a marriage is to maintain genuine love and satisfaction with your partner through positive affirmations.

When others perceive that the two of you are happily married, the likelihood of a third party trying to interject themselves into your marriage will be lower. In fact, people can sense when there is a rift between you and your husband, and the enemy is eagerly waiting to send someone in to proposition him—or you—to have an affair, causing further separation.

Your happiness and contentment with your husband can't be faked, and it will be crystal clear to lurkers and opportunists that you're not looking for a new partner or any hookups to fill a void. But again, making your marriage genuinely and noticeably enjoyable can only be done by affirming your spouse. And how do you do that? By talking about him publicly, frequently, and in a positive light.

8. Affirmation makes your husband into a leader.

Your husband is called to be a multifaceted leader—first to himself, secondly to his wife, and thirdly to his family. From there, is a leader to the outside world. But how can he be a truly effective leader in any of those areas if you aren't doing your part by *speaking life* to him?

Your status as a married woman carries weight, and while you may not occupy the leadership role that your husband is in, you still hold a position of leadership or influence in the lives of those around you. For example, your children, friend circle, or neighbors may all value your opinion and place a certain level of trust in you. And when they observe you speaking well of your spouse, that will inspire even more trust in you.

On the contrary, if every time your husband's name is brought up in a conversation, they hear a bickering complaint from you, then they're going to be more reserved in their communication with you. Because you speak negatively about the person you should value the most, they'll start thinking that you'll eventually do the same to them.

The moral here is that a man is only as good as the woman beside him. And even if he is a good man and a natural leader, the way you speak about him to others will influence their perspective of him, as well as the way they see you. If people see you praising your husband from a place of authentic admiration, they, too, are more willing to open up authentically with you.

Building a Stronger Marriage

It's been said that the key to a lasting relationship is communication. But what many relationship gurus who echo this aphorism don't expound on is how to *effectively* communicate.

Communication on its own, especially in the confines of a marriage or romantic union, is merely scratching the surface when it comes to building the foundation of a healthy relationship. Being a master communicator involves listening just as much as it does talking.

For a clearer understanding of what communication is all about, I like to use this definition from One Love, suggesting that communication is, "the successful conveying or sharing of ideas and feelings." And doing this in a healthy manner with a partner who reciprocates these attributes is what communication is all about (Mackler, 2018).

Since communication plays such a pivotal part in the success of any relationship—but especially in a marriage—here are a few pointers you can apply to be a more skillful communicator with your spouse:

Chapter 3:

Remember That Your Relationship With Him Predates Your Obligations to Your Children—and Will Outlive Them, Too

How Positive Speech Can Benefit Your Relationship

Parenting today looks worlds apart from what it was when some of our parents showed it to us. Decades back, there were clear representations of the tasks the husband and wife were each required to perform when it came to raising a family. Fathers were the main breadwinners and worked outside of the home, while mothers primarily took care of house chores and the children. And so, in most cases, "bringing home the bacon" was the only concern the father had—activities like helping with homework or taking turns doing the laundry were unheard of.

But today, things are markedly different. The idea of co-parenting has become more popular and accepted in our society, meaning that both parents are expected to be actively involved in the parenting process and to equally share household responsibilities. This ensures that equal effort is being given so that no one feels overwhelmed by the responsibilities of childrearing, home-running, or spouse-catering.

Identifying Your Passions, Skills, and Gifts

The fact that nowadays, in most marriages, both parents either work outside the home, or one parent works outside the home while one parent works from home, means that there is a wider range of options for catering to the children. When your children see that, despite their work situations, both parents still devote time to actively raising them, it sends them a positive message that their parents love each other enough to join forces for their sake. It even evokes a sense of balance and mutual respect, which your kids can one day carry into their own marriages.

But how do you juggle the responsibilities of co-parenting while remembering to nurture the foundational relationship that made the birth of children possible—*your marriage*? The co-parenting concept is beneficial in maintaining peace and stability because no one will begin to resent the other for their workload, or lack thereof. Indeed, the effectiveness of sensibly sharing the workload heavily depends on you and your husband's daily schedules, other commitments and responsibilities, as well as your gifts, passions, and preferences, according to Minno Life (Team, 2022).

This should also be taken into account because it helps to determine the strength and lasting affection of your marriage as you continue co-parenting. For example, your husband may be naturally good with children and possess a patient spirit that can effectively teach others. On the other hand, you may not possess the same level of patience when it comes to teaching children. Therefore, to alleviate frustration and ensure lasting peace, you may suggest he take the lead with homework and after-school studies.

Likewise, perhaps you're a stickler for a living environment that's neat and spotless, and as such, you may even gain a certain level of serenity from doing that. In contrast, your husband may not mind a bit of a mess and isn't as hard-pressed as you are when it comes to keeping his surroundings clean. You can therefore come to an agreement together on how to divide the household and childcare responsibilities. This way, you're using your natural gifts and talents to accomplish your parenting and household tasks efficiently and effectively.

Ensure That Your Schedule Aligns With Your Commitments

Balancing a demanding work schedule and equally demanding responsibilities at home will determine the harmony and longevity of your partnership. Finding ways to work around your schedule to accommodate your husband with work and raising children will be less strenuous for both of you. And this is precisely why you need to know what your schedule even allows you to commit to.

For example, if you've agreed to be a stay-at-home mom, then you'll obviously have more household and childrearing responsibilities because most of your time is spent, well, in the home around the children. But this doesn't mean the responsibilities of your working husband become obsolete. Because his work schedule outside the home is so demanding, he could be relegated to weekly or monthly tasks, as opposed to daily, such as taking out the garbage, mowing the lawn, or cleaning the windows.

But the same can also be said if he works at night. Together, you two can agree that he'll handle certain responsibilities during the day, such as grocery shopping or picking the children up from school in the afternoon, depending on the time his shift begins.

On the other hand, if your husband is a business owner or works from home, then you may need to figure out whether daytime or nighttime responsibilities would be more convenient for him. But depending on the field of business he's into, it should allow him a greater deal of flexibility in regard to evenly sharing the distribution of household responsibilities.

Whether you both work a typical day job, he works the night shift, or he runs a business from home, the goal is to ensure that you two are balancing the load as evenly as possible by using your unique gifts and strengths while fitting everything into your busy schedules.

The scripture that comes to mind for this topic of shared responsibilities between husband and wife is Ecclesiastes 4:9-10, which reads, "Two are better than one; because they have a good reward for their labor. For if they fall, the one will lift up his fellow: but woe to him that is alone when he falleth; for he hath not another to help him up again" (King James Bible Online, 1611b).

Let this be your inspiration to be each other's keeper by ensuring all these tasks don't fall solely on one person. When you've succeeded in striking this balance, you'll be able to enjoy the fruit of your marriage and family life much more comfortably.

Find Out What Your Spouse Needs From You

Now that we've covered you and your husband's individual gifts and passions, as well as how you both can allocate responsibilities and how you can both be helpful in maintaining your relationship, we're ready to move on to the next question: What does your spouse need from you? This is perhaps one of the most important questions we'll be tackling in this book. While doing your best to sustain the health of your relationship through the strategies we've covered thus far, a lot of the time, what's needed is basic communication.

That's right: Simply sitting with your husband and asking him what he needs from you is not only a way of getting a direct response from them, but it's also a way of expressing the "agape" love of God. Now, God's agape love is centered on sacrificing our own needs and desires for the sake of someone else. And this is the picture of what a Christian marriage should be: a willingness to lay down our lives for one another.

Another scripture that details this dynamic of God's love is found in Ephesians 5:24-25, which reads, "Therefore as the church is subject unto Christ, so let the wives be to their husbands in everything. Husbands love your wives, even as Christ loved the church, and gave himself for it" (King James Bible Online, 1611c).

In these verses of scripture, Paul is likening a Christian marriage between a man and woman to the relationship between Jesus Christ and the Church, which is the body of Christ. In verse 24, Paul states that women should be subject to their husbands in the same manner in which the Church is subject to Jesus. Now, you might be asking, "What does that even mean?"

Well, when the Church is in subjection to Christ, what that means, fundamentally, is that it follows His spiritual leadership as well as desires Him and His purposes in life to be accomplished. So, when you place this same definition in the context of a Christian marriage, it paints a picture of the way a wife should behave with her husband. By being subject to your husband, you're willing to submit to his spiritual leadership, and you have a deep desire for him and his purpose as a husband and father to be carried through.

However, take note that your subjection to your husband also bleeds into the next verse, which commands husbands to love their wives even as Christ loved the Church and sacrificed himself for it. Even though verse 25 is directed specifically at husbands, being subject to your husband is also an act of sacrifice. Because, let's face it, women in our modern world are encouraged to exercise their liberties by refusing to submit to their husbands, especially if they generate their own income. And so, by choosing to be subject to your husband and committing to the furtherance of his purpose, therein lies a great sacrifice.

Therefore, verse 25 is a call not only for husbands to love their wives in a sacrificial way as Christ loved the Church but also for wives to do the same. What's being said here, essentially, is that your husband is called to love you in a sacrificial way, and you are likewise called to return this sacrificial love to him. This is the way Christ intended for you to love each other. And by so doing, your marriage becomes an example to the world of the way Jesus loves.

Jesus Himself reiterates the need for us to be an example of his love in John 13:34-35, stating, "A new commandment I give unto you, That ye love one another; as I have loved you, that ye also love one another. By this shall all men know that ye are my disciples, if ye have love one to another."

In a world where divorce rates are high, and trust and faithfulness are lacking in relationships, people are looking for real, true love. So, when people behold you and your husband's willingness to serve each other in an authentic way, they'll be drawn to it, which will in turn lead them to Jesus Christ. That being said, be sure to ask your husband how you can tend to his needs, or in what ways you can lighten his load, both as a romantic partner and as a co-parent.

Take note, too, that this doesn't need to be an initiative that you embark on by yourself. Get your husband involved in planning out the ways in which you can both begin meeting each other's expectations.

Having unspoken expectations and then becoming distraught when those expectations aren't met keeps you and your husband in a perpetual state of dissatisfaction. But when you can come together, express your wants and needs, and also formulate a plan that's unique to your family dynamic, then you'll begin to see your marriage union thrive in the midst of fulfilling your commitments as parents.

Keeping Your Relationship Alive While Raising Children

There has been a common misconception in modern marriages that once children come into the picture, they automatically become the focal point, leaving the spousal relationship to wither away. And sure, the immediate well-being of your children should be prioritized, along with making preparations for their futures. But making your lives all about the children at the expense of your marriage is guaranteed to result in the loss of both your spouse and children.

Both you and your husband could be guilty of putting your marriage on the back burner for the sake of your children.

However, since this book is geared toward wives, I would like to give you a few solid reasons as to why you shouldn't make the mistake of putting your children before your marriage, according to All Pro Dad (Maul, 2022).

1. You married your husband, not your children.

As the mother who carried the children during pregnancy and ultimately gave birth to them, you automatically have a much closer attachment to them. As a result, the temptation to give more of your time, attention, and affection to them while neglecting your husband is very prevalent. But you should be reminded of the fact that you made your marriage vows to your husband—not to your children.

And so when you give your children precedence over your husband (although he's a large part of the reason they're alive and healthy), you're actually dishonoring your union. By putting each other first, in contrast, you're creating an environment that enables love to flourish, and in turn, gives the children a sense of security.

2. Love your spouse for the sake of your children.

Expressing love for your spouse, especially in the presence of your children, encourages a feeling of safety. By choosing to love your husband, you're teaching them what a healthy, stable relationship is supposed to look like between a man and a woman. And it's for this reason that, regardless of the arguments and disagreements that are bound to arise with your husband, you should strongly resist speaking about him negatively in the presence of your children.

3. Marriage is the foundation of the family.

This brings us to the next reason why you should put your marriage before your kids—the foundation of the family. Indeed, your family is supported by the preservation of your marriage, because without it, everything would fall apart. And so, dismissing or ignoring the problems in your marriage under the guise of focusing on the children is actually the greatest disservice you could do to your kids. Trying to maintain a family in the midst of a broken marriage is like trying to build a house on a cracked foundation—when the foundation fails, the family crumbles.

4. Your marriage is more impactful than you realize.

Even when you try to mask the underlying tension you and your husband might be feeling due to a misunderstanding, your children are highly perceptive and can pick up on problems between the two of you. And as such, the stability of your marriage could affect their performance at school, their overall demeanor, as well as their present and future relationships—for better or for worse.

Your marital issues can be especially detrimental to your children if they have been accustomed to experiencing the stability of a healthy marriage. A sudden shift that threatens extremities like separation or divorce will immediately be felt by the children, having a negative impact on their emotional and psychological well-being.

5. Your children will mirror what they see.

According to Edutopia, the most critical phase of a child's ability to retain knowledge and form intelligence is between the ages of two and seven (Sriram, 2020). Of course, children will still mimic your behavior after age seven, but the earliest stages are the most crucial because that's when they emulate the behavior of their parents the most.

When they observe sacrificial love, affection, patience, kindness, gentleness, forgiveness, and respect, they are bound to adopt these virtues. Furthermore, as these virtues become embedded into their character, they'll begin to reflect them out into the world.

But, sadly, the opposite can also just as easily happen. If your kids are exposed to constant fighting, anger, selfishness, and hatred between you and your husband at an early age, they will also feed off of this negative energy, adopt it as part of their character, and return it to the world.

6. Marriage is for life.

If you neglect to nurture your marriage after your children are born, and you and your spouse stay together until the children get older and move out, you're most likely going to find yourselves living more like strangers than lovers in your empty home.

That's why it's so important to maintain the romance and passion in your relationship while raising your children. When you've each done your job as parents and the children have grown into adults, your spouse will be the only one living with you.

Like a wise entrepreneur, you need to invest love and respect into your relationship at each and every stage of your married life, so that even in old age, you'll still be reaping the fruits of your labor.

Prioritizing Your Spousal Relationship

Simply put, if you want to keep your grass green, you're going to have to water it. The grass, in this context, is your marriage. But what tends to happen when children are introduced into the family dynamic is that you become so preoccupied with watering the other pastures of life (besides the kids, there are jobs, careers, pets, money, and health that come to mind) that you neglect the need to water and nourish your marriage. And of course, whatever you fail to water, over time, slowly begins to die.

The same, unfortunately, can be applied to your marriage. The less you invest in the romantic nature of your marriage, the more likely you are to lose your connection with your husband. So, before all hope is lost, let's go over a few steps to building a more loving relationship even while devoting your time to parenthood:

- Schedule time to talk about your goals and dreams as a couple. It's important to have a joint vision, and to follow up with each other, ensuring that you're both on the same trajectory.

- Remind each other that you're riding out this marriage until the wheels fall off. Divorce wasn't in the plan when the two of you got married, and while you may not always have the time and energy to sit down and talk about your marriage, it's important that you both agree to set time aside to build the relationship.

- Communicate your thoughts and feelings honestly and frequently. Being vulnerable builds intimacy, and if you both have busy schedules, you can still accomplish this through emails, sticky notes, and social media messages.

- Try to resurrect the feelings you had for your partner when the marriage was fresh. When the monotony of housework creates an atmosphere of boring routines, try spicing things up with your husband by doing some of the things that got sparks flying at the start of the marriage.

- Shut off the TV and put down the smartphone. Again, the entrapment of daily routines can lead you to get lost in a Lifetime movie or spend time scrolling social media. If you turn off the electronic devices at night, you'll be able to focus more on your partner and engage each other in lighthearted conversation.

- Do you and your husband share a hobby or interest? Whether it's hiking, cycling, playing a sport, singing karaoke, or shooting paintball guns, enjoy it together! If you haven't found a shared interest, then start probing each other to see what you find.

- Love deeply and forgive easily. Don't let your partner's quirks and minor problems upset you. Master the art of letting go, especially if it's in regard to mistakes or negative behaviors that triggered you. And don't say that you forgive your husband for something he did and then proceed to constantly remind him of it every chance you get. That'll only make matters worse and prove that you haven't truly forgiven him. If there is something bothering you that you want to address, do so in a loving manner, and try to start each day with a clean slate.

- Every family has its own set of issues, but the trials you face together should draw you closer as you find solutions to your problems together. You could be going through a season of drought as a family—maybe your husband lost his job, a business deal went bad, or there is a sudden illness in the family. Instead of pointing the finger at your husband in a desperate attempt to find answers, try being kind, understanding, and reassuring. It's only through these trials that you will realize how valuable your partner is and how much you need each other.

- Turn everyday tasks into special moments with your husband. Whether the two of you are out shopping for groceries or at home doing chores, there's always an opportunity to make your time together more fun while getting things done.

- Make a concerted effort to be loving, kind, and affectionate toward each other in front of your children. Of course, this should not be forced—rather, it should come across genuinely and effortlessly in conversation. This includes giving each other compliments and showing gratitude. This way, the children will learn appreciation for the efforts of others as well as how to be grateful.

I truly hope that these tips on prioritizing your marriage will inspire you to place more emphasis on your love connection with your husband. After all, it existed before your children were born—and if you tend to it carefully, it will still be there once your kids are gone. If there is one single thing to take away from this chapter, it's that your marriage is the foundation upon which your family is built. Always remember that, and always make sure it's as secure as possible.

We'll now be moving on to Chapter 4, which will center around your appreciation and acknowledgment of your husband's efforts to provide for you and your children.

Chapter 4:

Appreciate and Give Him Credit for His Provision, Regardless of How He Obtained It

Show Appreciation for Your Husband's Provision

Each romantic relationship is defined by its own set of characteristics, but when it comes to the reasons why partners fall out of love, it's usually always the same. And while it's also common for both partners to blame each other for why the relationship fell through the cracks, rarely does either one ever take the time to assess how their own actions may have been a contributing factor to its demise.

The truth is that healthy relationships require a lot of hard work to be maintained. During the honeymoon phase, both partners are basking in the blissfulness of newfound romance, the season where most consider themselves to be "in love." But most aren't aware of the thin line that separates being "*in* love" from being "*out* of love," and the reason for this is that it's not easily identifiable.

As your marriage becomes settled, there are habits and behavioral patterns that you may begin to develop over time that slowly take the relationship to the "out of love" zone. But while these behaviors are often hard to read, they can be recognized if you know exactly what to look for. One of the main reasons why people eventually check out of their relationships is a lack of appreciation.

While both men and women are prone to feeling this in a relationship, men in particular, being less emotional than women, tend to feel unappreciated much more due to the many invaluable qualities they offer to the relationship. But this is just one of the reasons that would cause your spouse to begin falling out of love. Taken from Hey Sigmund, we'll cover that, as well as some of the other reasons that your love life may be on the decline (Young, 2015).

Lack of Appreciation

The emotional currency, like any other form of currency, needs to be replenished whenever it's been spent. The time, energy, and attention that was invested into the relationship to get it going in the beginning will still need to be invested as the years go by. Sure, you may indeed love and respect your husband deep inside, but you can't expect him to "know" that you love him based on the past experiences you shared.

If you were both openly loving, affectionate, and appreciative of each other at the beginning of the relationship, then this is what will be needed to continually nourish the relationship. This level of openness and vulnerability is what makes your relationship different from any other in your life.

Healthy marriages—and romantic relationships in general—have a natural rhythm of give-and-take, and furthermore, they also experience moments of highs and lows. These changes in momentum affect where the relationship may fall on your priority list. Because of the other demands of life, it may be at the top of that list at certain times, while at others, it may be on the back burner.

With the preoccupation of our lives, this is to be expected. However, if your marriage is important to you, it shouldn't remain at the bottom of your priority list for too long. I've learned in life and in marriage that no matter how busy your schedule may be, you'll always make time for the things that you prioritize.

Another important aspect of appreciating your spouse is the fact that you wouldn't allow him to pour his love, care, and adoration into you without reciprocating it. Here, both acknowledgement and appreciation are key, because if you were sensitive to your husband's actions, you would acknowledge them. And after your acknowledgment, you would begin to appreciate his efforts and reciprocate his gestures.

If one person in the relationship is constantly giving, and thus filling up someone else's cup, then eventually, the giver will run dry. And when the giver becomes exhausted and no one else is pouring back into their cup, the relationship begins to implode. In short, it takes equal effort from both partners to make a marriage work.

So, if one person continuously puts in the effort to make the marriage work, they'll begin to feel insignificant to the other, and as such, their emotional currency will be spent due to a lack of appreciation and reciprocation.

If you've been taking your husband for granted and now you notice he's begun emotionally disconnecting from you, then here are some tips to keep the flame of passion burning between the two of you:

- Acknowledge his efforts, especially the little things.
- Tell him the qualities you love about him.

- Show gratitude by being thankful often.

- Joyfully cater to him.

- Be affectionate.

- Say your "good mornings" and "goodnights" as though he's the reason those mornings and nights are good.

- Compliment and shower him with love when in public.

- Kiss him slowly, passionately, and frequently.

The Emotional Connection Is Nonexistent

A great deal of the best marriages and relationships are those that started out as friendships. But, so often, marriages are formed through hot and heavy romantic interaction, with lots of sensuality and romantic passion involved. While sexual attraction and romance are necessary for a budding romantic relationship or marriage, this is actually a faulty foundation to build upon if you intend to have a lasting marriage.

Why is that, you ask? Well, it's because sensual passion can only hold a marriage together for so long. When you've done all there is to do in the bedroom, what's left? It's been proven that the intense love and passion that is experienced during the honeymoon phase begins to fizzle away after two years, at which point the emotional connection of a genuine friendship is what would sustain the relationship.

Being able to connect emotionally is what truly defines whether or not a marriage will last. It allows for a mature and loving relationship to take over when the bedroom passion starts to fade. That isn't to say that you and your husband will no longer be passionate in the bedroom, but rather, your friendship will allow you to get through the dry spells of intimacy, naturally rebuilding the momentum.

If your husband takes the time to rebuild an emotional connection with you, don't take it for granted. And if there never was an emotional connection to begin with, then here are some ways to reignite that fire:

- Engage in regular conversation.
- Call just to check-in.
- When asking about his day, be genuinely interested in his response.
- Listen proactively when he speaks.
- Be attentive to his moods and acknowledge his emotions.
- Cultivate an atmosphere of joy and laughter with him.
- Be invested in what's going on in his world and don't assume you already know.
- Be his peace at home from the chaos in the world.
- Let your guard down and allow yourself to be soft with him.

Dispel Boredom With Spontaneity

If you and your husband have been married for some time now, chances are you're familiar with his personality and he knows yours. In many relationships, there exists a perfect balance of one partner who is high-energy, enthusiastic, and spontaneous, while the other is reserved, cautious, and less outgoing. A balanced pair such as this usually prevents boredom from taking root in a long-term relationship or marriage, but when children are involved, even the best-paired relationships can be at risk of falling into stale habits.

However, let's suppose your husband is the exciting and charismatic one in the relationship—the one who is always investing emotionally. And as such, you've grown accustomed to this. It follows, then, that when he's depleted emotionally, it'll be up to you to pour back into him so that the relationship doesn't begin to wane. Even if you're the reserved type, try something a little out of the ordinary to get him going, like one of the following:

- Surprise him by making his favorite dish or dessert.

- Plan a romantic evening at home and include his favorite bottle of wine or champagne.

- Sit with him and watch his favorite movie or TV show, and have a genuinely good time doing it.

- Hang out together and truly enjoy each other's company.

- Plan a date for the two of you with a list of his favorite restaurants to choose from.

- Plan a day at the spa where both of you can relax and get cozy.

These simple yet thoughtful gestures will convey your consideration and appreciation for your husband's efforts as your financial, emotional, and spiritual provider.

Appreciate His Physical Intimacy

They say you never know what you have until it's gone, or in some cases until it's been discontinued. And when physical intimacy in a marriage has been discontinued (for whatever reason), then the relationship might be on the verge of collapse.

Now, keep in mind that physical intimacy doesn't always have to take the shape of a sexual encounter. After all, as you'll recall, it takes much more than sex to keep a marriage together. There's another form of physical intimacy that involves affectionate touching, which can be as simple as lightly touching your husband's back when you pass, or offering a caressing massage while he lies down.

These nonsexual forms of physical intimacy have been found to increase long-term happiness in a relationship, and skin-to-skin touching has also been found to release the same chemicals in the brain as sex, such as dopamine, endorphins, and oxytocin. Further research, according to Hey Sigmund, has revealed that humans have a built-in antenna that is able to interpret emotional messages via touch only.

Through nonsexual physical intimacy, love and trust can be communicated between romantic partners, which is why intimate relationships are so different from any other kind. Therefore, if your husband withdraws his physical intimacy toward you due to feeling unappreciated or undervalued, it could mark the beginning of the loss of emotional intimacy in your marriage.

Normally, when a spouse withholds physical intimacy, in any form, from their partner, they're more than likely fulfilling their physical and emotional needs elsewhere. So, aside from the financial provision your husband supplies, be grateful just for his manly physical presence. You never know how blessed you are to have someone sleep next to you, playfully tease you, caress you, and affectionately kiss you until they're no longer doing those things.

Of course, if your husband has withheld physical intimacy with you, and you desire to bring it back, these are some of the things you can do:

- Start complimenting him and recognizing the little things he does.

- Let him know that you appreciate the things he used to do as a means of restoring the emotional connection.

- Initiate incidental touching with him at least 10 times a day, starting small with light brushes. Over time, turn up the heat with deliberate touches, like holding hands or placing your hand on his shoulder.

Strengthening Appreciation in Marriage

Before we get into what gratitude is and how recognizing your husband's efforts can result in a happier marriage, we're going to briefly focus our attention on the archnemesis of gratitude—criticism.

Gary Chapman of Symbis Assessment says this about critical spouses: "People tend to criticize their spouse most loudly in the area where they themselves have the deepest emotional need" (Les, 2017). Having an overly critical spouse can be one

64

of the most stifling experiences any man can go through in his marriage. Criticism, in general, usually stems from a need to control and micromanage the actions or habits of others.

Now, if you're being honest with yourself and find that you have been extremely critical of your husband, you should know that these criticisms are capable of completely crippling the intimacy in your marriage. That's because when you criticize your husband, you're demoralizing him by making him feel incapable and invaluable, despite his best efforts to make a healthy contribution to the relationship.

How would you feel if after trying your very best to accommodate your husband, you were met with harsh criticism over what you didn't do correctly or could have done better, instead of showing gratitude for the efforts you made? Undoubtedly, this would break your spirit and leave you devastated.

This is exactly how your husband feels when you choose to point out every perceived flaw that you believe he has. Has your husband ever referred to you as a "control freak?" That's because your proclivity to critique every little thing he does comes across as a need to constantly dictate your immediate surroundings—which includes him.

You may think that your criticisms of your husband are coming from a place of wanting things to be done "properly." Indeed, you may think they stem from routine tasks around the house to the way he parents the children, down to the way he manages his finances. If you think that your way is always the right way to do things, then there's no way you can truly be grateful for anything he does.

In particular, if you're struggling in the area of being a control freak, you should know that this comes from a place of having a high level of unconscious anxiety, which manifests itself as a need to get control of your world. Your world, of course, would include your immediate environment and the people in it, which, in most cases, involves your husband and children.

In order to remedy your anxious behavior so that it doesn't drive a wedge in the emotional connection with your husband, you first need to acknowledge the inner anxiety that fuels this controlling nature. Once you've identified and accepted the root cause of your controlling nature, you'll need to sit down with your husband and talk about the issue.

Once you have discussed the root of the problem, know that it most likely won't go away after one conversation. However, acknowledge at the same time that it will allow your husband to have a bit more grace when dealing with you. And over time, as the two of you converse more about your anxiety, you may find that it eases the tension in your relationship, and your critical nature might also be alleviated.

Showing Gratitude in Your Marriage

With a brief overview of how compulsive criticism can deteriorate the emotional intimacy in your marriage, I'll now detail another way to combat this trait, which is through gratitude. When your anxiety is giving you a million different reasons to find fault in your husband or to critique something he's done, pause and think of all the things to be grateful for.

According to an article from Positive Psychology,

> Gratitude turns what little you have to abundance.
>
> Gratitude is so much more than saying thank you.
>
> Gratitude changes your perspective of your world (Ackerman, 2017).

Gratitude is a very similar emotion to appreciation, and the two are often used interchangeably. But gratitude, in particular, is described as the sense of happiness and thankfulness one feels in response to receiving good fortune or a treasured tangible gift.

While appreciation is defined as the recognition and delight of the good qualities of someone or something, gratitude is defined as being both an emotional state and a trait. What this means is that one can feel gratitude for someone or something at a particular moment in time, while simultaneously, gratitude can also be experienced in the long term as a positive character trait.

The same article from Positive Psychology goes on to reveal that there are two stages involved in the feeling of gratitude:

1. The acknowledgment of goodness in your life brings about the affirmation that life is ultimately good and worth living. We are gratified by the acknowledgment of having received something good, as well as by the effort the giver has put into what we've received.

2. We also experience gratitude when we recognize that the sources of this goodness are found outside of ourselves. This inspires us to be grateful to the Creator, other people, the world, nature, and all that is around us.

Here, we see that the two stages of gratitude encompass our recognition of the goodness in our lives followed by the recognition of the source by which the goodness came.

So, the next step would be for you to apply the feeling of gratitude in your marriage, especially in regard to your husband. Do you acknowledge that his presence is a force of good in your life? If yes, are you grateful to God first and to your husband second for the value that he brings to your life?

Showing gratitude for your husband's achievements and efforts can have transformative effects on your marriage. It can make you more cognizant of the way you verbalize your appreciation as well as in the way you show it. Showing gratitude to your husband can also make you less judgmental, so instead of actively looking for ways to find fault in his character or in his efforts, you'll be more inclined to praise him, which communicates a greater level of respect.

More Strategies for Showing Gratitude

Earlier, I highlighted a few tips on how to restore emotional connection with your husband by expressing your appreciation for the ways in which he provides for you. As you'll recall, these can be financial, physical, emotional, spiritual, and so on. But now, we're going to go more in-depth with some of the additional strategies you can employ for conveying gratitude for his provision.

Make a Commitment to Your Relationship

If you're the critical type who's always looking for the wrong in what your partner has done, then there's a high possibility that you might be considering the tempting possibility that the grass is greener on the other side. Indeed, when you can only think of your husband's worst qualities and you start viewing your marriage as unbearable, that's when you start entertaining the idea that life outside of your marriage might be worth the risk.

But, as we concluded before, the constant criticism of your husband stems from a place of anxiety, which is then expressed as a need to be in control and have things done your way. But if you can shift your perspective from discrediting your husband's actions because they're not done to your supposed "higher standard," to being grateful for his unique qualities that attracted you to him to begin with, then looking outside won't be an option.

Complimenting your husband's star qualities with genuine admiration is one excellent way of expressing gratitude for him. And when you come to the realization that he possesses all the traits you claim to want in a husband, then divorce or adultery won't even be worth considering. You need to decide ahead of time in your marriage to remove divorce from the table, as well as to commit to making your marriage stronger, rather than exaggerating your husband's faults and looking outside of the marriage for answers.

Offer Your Assistance

It's one thing to say that you're grateful for all your partner does, but it's another thing to put action behind those words. If you take the time to really empathize with your partner after realizing all that he has to do as a man, you'll be more than willing to offer your help in alleviating some of the stress. A man will rarely complain about his duties as a man because, simply put, that's just what he's required to do. And though you may not be able to truly put yourself in his shoes, you can still show your gratitude by doing things he doesn't enjoy in his stead, like taking out the trash once in a while or helping him maintain the lawn.

Honor His Feelings

Most husbands today complain that they don't feel heard or understood by their wives, and their feelings are often dismissed. Everyone has a unique way of expressing themselves, whether through words or actions, and your husband is no exception. We know that effective communication is the key to a functioning relationship, right?

So when your husband is trying to communicate feelings of excitement, disappointment, neglect, or any other emotion, it's wise to honor those feelings.

In fact, you should practice gratitude for the very fact that he's even trying to communicate those feelings with you. Again, it takes a lot for men to open up emotionally, and so when he does so with you and your response is dismissive, it can be seen as a betrayal. When you don't honor your husband's feelings, he can respond in either one of two ways:

1. He will shut down emotionally and become cold and distant.

2. He will become tempted to confide in people and/or places where his feelings are being honored.

Mail a Card

It doesn't matter if you're mailing a written card to your own address—simply do the unexpected by writing a message to your partner in the form of a love letter expressing your gratitude for him and emphasizing how much you care about him. If you're a shy person who is unable to openly express their feelings, mailing a letter to your husband, or even sending him an email, is a thoughtful yet simple way of letting him know your truest feelings. It also shows that you respect him enough to find a way to express yourself to him, even though it may not be your strong point.

Try Each Other's Interests

You and your husband are two completely unique people with separate personalities, likes, dislikes, hobbies, and interests. And that's exactly what makes your union so effervescent. As a way to deepen the emotional connection between the two of you as well as be grateful for each other's idiosyncrasies, you can make a list of the things your husband enjoys doing in his leisure time. From there, offer to accompany him on those outings as a show of support and genuine interest in him. You can also make a list of your own interests and invite him to participate in those with you as well.

Respect His Personality

Again, no two people are the same—I can't stress that enough. Although the Bible says in Genesis 2:24 that "[...] a man shall leave his father and mother, and shall cleave unto his wife: and they shall be one flesh," it goes without saying that your husband has his own set of personality traits that makes him unique, and so do you. You may have even realized that God, in His perfect wisdom, designed your husband's personality with certain strengths that balance out your weaknesses—and vice versa.

Therefore, his passions, emotions, and behaviors can act as a complimentary part of your life so that you bring out the best in each other. However, just as you may love and cherish his positive traits, you may also loathe other aspects of his personality. Nevertheless, you should learn to respect all facets of your husband's personality.

Live in the Moment

If you're actively invested in bettering your relationship, then it's best to take it one day at a time. Try not to focus so much on the possibilities that the future holds by asking *what-if* questions. Instead, use your energy to focus on the progress you and your husband are making in the present moment. Ultimately, the joint action you take to improve the quality of your marriage today will set the foundation for the longevity of your union.

Society has instigated a trend of shaming men who work traditional blue-collar jobs Indeed, manual work such as that undertaken by factory workers, construction workers, miners, electricians, plumbers, mechanics, and so on, is generally frowned upon today. In our ever-increasing digital age of technology, there are many ways to make a living without having to do manual work, such as social media influencing, media marketing, web designing, and software developing. When it comes down to it, neither kind of job should be shamed. An employed man is one who provides for his family, regardless of the specifics of his job.

However your husband makes a living, whether by primarily using his mind or his muscles, you should be grateful and supportive of his means of provision. Going back to the issue of respect, the fact that he is actually assuming his rightful position as the leader and provider in your life should be enough to earn your utmost respect. Would you rather have a man who obtains provision for you and your family with his mind or muscles, or one who does nothing at all and depends on you to be the provider?

Again, respecting the financial provision of your husband falls under the umbrella of all other forms of provision (physical, emotional, or spiritual). But in order to be truly respectful of all that he provides, you need to be appreciative of those things so that the emotional and physical intimacy won't be hindered.

And now, as we head into Chapter 5, you want to ensure that you're keeping yourself grounded in the reality of what a godly marriage looks like. Case in point, godly marriages aren't described in romantic dramas, TV soap operas, or romance novels. If your marriage is meant to honor God, then marriages described outside of God's design shouldn't be considered as an option to model your marriage after. Without further ado, let's pick this right up in the next chapter.

Chapter 5:

Stop Reading Romance Novels

The Fairy-Tale Expectations of Romance Novels

I'm sorry to say, but for the sake of your marriage, it may be best to let these go. Seriously.

We've all been fed the unrealistic expectation of romantic relationships and marriages from a tender age in the form of our favorite childhood stories—Cinderella, Snow White and the Seven Dwarfs, Sleeping Beauty, Rapunzel, Beauty and the Beast, and many others. Film adaptations, both live-action and animated, have been made out of these fairy-tale stories, which have kept this fantasy alive in our minds well into adulthood.

These fairy tales—and the fanciful ideas about love and marriage that stem from them—have a particular effect on women. In fact, many women who modeled their romantic experiences around fairy tales in childhood tend to keep the idea alive through romantic novels in their adulthood, adding to their unrealistic imaginative supposition.

Some people seem to forget that many, if not all, of these romance novels are fictional chronicles, conceptualized by an author who has been fed the same fantasy of false expectations and is now selling that fantasy to hopeless romantics. Whether the author wholeheartedly believes in their own romanticized reveries, or they are well aware of the improbability of the stories they're pushing, they're making money off of a falsehood—and you're spending money to fall for it.

Again, it's a harsh truth, and I hate to knock a hobby of yours you might thoroughly enjoy, but I stand by this condemnation. In fact, the Times of India provides us with some uncomfortable truths about the effects these beloved romance novels are having on relationships in real life (Timesofindia.com, 2023). Below, we'll go over some of these in detail:

Unrealistic Expectations

How many women are still waiting for a handsome and wealthy prince to stumble upon them by a stroke of fate and save them from a life of misery? To put it bluntly, fairy tales consumed in childhood lead to this exact kind of folly. You may be shocked by the insurmountable number of women who have genuinely set this kind of expectation for their real-life love story. Worse yet is the fact that many of these women awaiting their rich prince charming may already be married. As you may be familiar with yourself, such romance stories and novels are skilled at depicting idealistic relationships with flawless partners who sweep the damsels off their feet in grandiose style.

Readers then tend to place themselves in these scenarios, which leads to unreasonable expectations about love and romance. And if they're already in a relationship, then dissatisfaction may begin to set in as they compare their own life and relationship to what is being portrayed in the novel. If you're a reader who isn't able to separate fact from fiction, then your dissatisfaction may lead you to seek a partner or relationship more attuned to the one in the novel. Perhaps worse yet, you may apply pressure on your husband to become the suave knight in shining armor who has now captivated your mind.

Encouraged Escapism

Similar to the way that many people spend hours scrolling through social media, fascinated with the lives of celebrities as a way to escape their own reality, those who read romance novels also engage in a form of escapism. The excitement and passion in romance novels immerse you in a fantasy world that, oftentimes, is starkly different from your real life. And just like the previous point, it causes dissatisfaction and ingratitude when comparisons are made between the lives of the characters in the novel and their own existence.

Inspiring Creativity

Don't get me wrong: Not all the effects of reading romance novels are detrimental to your marriage. In fact, if you're reading from a rational perspective, these love stories may actually inspire creative ideas that can add a touch of romance and suspense to your marriage, encouraging you to express love for your partner in innovative ways. But, remember, you must be someone with a rational mind who isn't swayed by the fictional unrealistic expectations within the book. If not, you may start placing those unrealistic expectations on your partner, which would eventually put a strain on the relationship if he doesn't measure up.

Enhanced Communication

Of course, the most satisfying romance novels are those written by skilled wordsmiths who have a profound understanding of the dynamics of romantic relationships, emotions, everyday scenarios, and communication. And as such, another positive aspect of reading romance novels is that they can enhance your effective communication, empathy, and emotional intelligence skills. In short, if you struggle in the area of communication, applying some of the banter you read in these novels could enhance your marriage by improving your communication skills.

Deeper Intimacy

Aside from potentially enhancing communication with your partner, romance novels are also renowned for their ability to provide highly descriptive, erotic scenes of physical intimacy. Again, the reader must use wisdom as this can also create unrealistic expectations that jeopardize the foundation of your relationship. However, on a positive note, romance novels can teach you how to explore your partner's love language, exciting ways to please your husband intimately, as well as how you should appeal to his masculine sexual nature.

Also, if your marriage is based on a godly foundation, you must discern whether the sexual descriptions in the novel are within the confines of your Christian beliefs. Before endorsing what you've learned, consider seeking consent from your partner.

As you can see, there are definitely some nuanced pros and cons when talking about the seemingly compulsive interest in romance novels. But ultimately, many would argue that, with the often sexually explicit, passionately erotic descriptions being published in these books, the level of sexual fantasy they create in the minds of their readers rivals even the graphic depictions of pornography.

The Impact of Emotional Porn

According to Sweet Savage Flame, a whopping 82% of romance novel readers are women in their early 40s (Diaz. 2023). This leaves only 18% of the readers as men, which recently increased in 2014 with the release of the *Fifty Shades* film series. But that still doesn't come close to the staggering percentage of women who make up the buyers in the world of romantic fiction. In fact, romantic fiction accounts for 55% of the revenue of all fiction books, generating an estimated $1.44 billion in 2022 alone, which is an increase from the $1.35 billion in revenue from 2014.

What makes romance novels so addictive, especially to women, is the ultra-idealistic premise of two people falling hopelessly in love, like a picture-perfect love story. Not to mention the steamy sex scenes that encourage both male and female readers to indulge in their deepest sexual fantasies. But, again, parallels have been made between the sexual fantasies that are produced by romance novels and full-blown pornography, which then brings into question the spiritual detriment of romance novels.

Now, some may wonder how such a parallel can exist between two genres that seem worlds apart in the magnitude of their impact on consumers. But according to Iowa State Daily, researchers Ogi Ogas and Sai Gaddam behind the book, *A Billion Wicked Thoughts*, deduced that the major difference between romance novels and pornography was found in the base depiction of the idea of "true love" (Liu, 2014).

Firstly, the main objective in pornography is the fulfillment of the male's desire, which is achieved by depicting a gorgeous woman, robust in every appealing part of the body, being brought to pleasure by his physical prowess and sexual dominance. Pornography's appeal to the male psyche is reflected in the relatively high percentage of American men who consume this content, which is around 69%, compared to the percentage of women, which is approximately 40% in a given year (Smith and LeSuesur, 2023).

On the other hand, in romance fiction, the reader's emotions and pathos are evoked based on the storylines found in these novels, which follow the heroine developing unbridled feelings for her knight in shining armor, who is almost always depicted as the typical alpha male. To give him an element of edginess and mystique, he is often defined as having a harrowing past, stemming from lots of money, and being physically appealing. In the mind of most women, this would be the description of the ideal male archetype whom they would undoubtedly marry, which becomes the main objective of the heroine in the story.

Both scenarios delude men and women into thinking that pleasing or taming the opposite sex is a matter of bedroom showmanship or utilizing feminine wiles, as showcased in both the literary and visual genres of fiction. In either case, there is a false assumption of expectations set for both genders, which can lead to a breakdown in relationships due to a disconnect with reality.

However, contrary to popular belief, it's not the X-rated raunchy sex scenes in romance novels that prove to cause potential damage to the relationships of the women who read them. The real danger, according to Psychologist Julia Slattery, who has encountered a number of patients diagnosed as clinically addicted to romance novels, was found in the fact that the women who engage in reading romance novels become discontented with their relationships because they derive greater stimulation from the novels.

So, the more these women read about the idealistic love and alpha male archetypal partner, the less they feel connected to their partners in real life. This, then, can lead to a complete replacement of their partner for the emotional connection they now have to the romance novels. And obviously, the lack of emotional connection will begin to erode the relationship, leading to separation or divorce.

A similar outcome occurs in men who view pornography. In short, they become addicted to the dopamine released in their brain. Furthermore, thanks to the internet, the ease of access to which pornography is made available has made attaining sexual arousal extremely easy. Addiction, sadly, soon follows.

According to Medium, the instant gratification that comes with watching pornography is akin to the instantaneous high that one gets after snorting cocaine, which is also what makes cocaine highly addictive (Kowalski, 2020). When the feeling of euphoria wears off after watching pornography, it sends users in search of another hit of dopamine.

This can also characterize the neural response of women who are addicted to reading romance novels. Because a sense of emotional satisfaction is derived from these novels, the bodily sensations that stem from the chemical release ultimately rewire their brains to associate romance fiction novels with feelings of "love."

Giving Up Romance Fiction Can Lead to Greater Intimacy in Marriage

With all this said, it becomes second nature for women to turn to romance novels for an emotional connection—especially when there is instability in their marriage. Some female romance readers even prefer to stay single, substituting an actual companion for the comfort they receive from romance novels.

Thus, an addiction is formed because there is an emotional void that needs to be filled, and stories of an unrealistic love life do just the trick. Meanwhile, these stories also give them an escape from the reality of their singlehood. And again, married women are not exempt from this addiction either, as they would also be looking for an escape from their reality if their actual lives seemed to pale in comparison to the excitement in these romance novels.

Similarly to the hard drugs I've mentioned, romance novels can act as a numbing agent to the problems you face in your marriage. Indeed, if you've been reading these novels as a way of escaping from your marriage problems, it's important to realize that these novels simply aren't real. What *is* real, of course, is your marriage.

Failure to deal with your vulnerabilities and the insecurities within your marriage will leave you in a cycle of denial and depression. And trying to recreate your marriage according to the standards of the unrealistic expectations set by society and romance novels isn't going to change anything for the better.

So, in order to correct the disrespect you may be showing your husband, as well as the disharmony in your marriage, it's time to get real about the happily-ever-after illusion you've been sold by these romance stories. Think of all that is expected of modern relationships, and think of how the media perpetuates these expectations. Perhaps some disappointments you have with your marriage stem from the ridiculous expectations that romance novels and other forms of popular media are promoting? It's certainly worth musing over.

If you've created a habit of turning to the escapism of romance novels, then maybe it's time to address your problems head-on and work through them with your husband. He may not be the epitome of masculinity when judged by the fictional standards of romance novels, but if he's determined to lead a godly life in a godly marriage, then he's as masculine as they come in the real world.

Yes, it's true that as a woman, you may enjoy the world of fantasy that romance novels envelop you in, but you should remember that fantasies don't bring with them real-life consequences. If you wish for a more respectful, long-lasting marriage with your husband that guarantees genuine satisfaction, then you may want to seriously consider putting a stop to reading romance novels.

Nurturing a Fulfilling Relationship

Once the substitutes for the emotional connection between you and your husband are eliminated, you should begin to work on restoring that emotional connection naturally.

Depending on how deeply invested you have been in reading romance novels, it may require a detoxification process to wean yourself off of the addiction, just as it would with pornography. What this looks like is possibly having to rebuild the emotional connection with your husband from the ground up, especially if the romance novels have been your primary source of emotional intimacy for some time now.

Truly, women should be held to the same level of accountability in regard to consuming emotional pornography through reading romance novels as men are to watching pornography. There's a plethora of scientific arguments made suggesting that, because of the psychological, emotional, and physical effects of porn, men need to give it up in order to truly appreciate sex with their monogamous partner. Likewise, because of the potential risk of escapism, emotional detachment, and unrealistic expectations caused by reading romance novels, wives who wish to enjoy a more fulfilling monogamous marriage must also be willing to give up their addiction to emotional porn.

As I stated previously, not everything about romantic novels should be viewed through a darkened lens. When utilized correctly, you could actually enhance the quality of certain areas of your marriage by subtly applying some of the skills you learned in the novels. For example, if you have encountered problems with communication between you and your spouse,

83

then adopting some of the communication styles and emotional finesse in your marriage could actually prove effective.

If, perhaps, you were more shy and reserved when it came to communicating your wants and needs, then by applying what you learned about the complexities of relationships from reading the novels, you can begin to enhance your emotional intelligence. As we know, communication is the key to a healthy and thriving relationship, and a larger percentage of our communication is done emotionally and through nonverbal cues. And so, getting a firm grasp on communication can be an ideal way of nurturing your relationship back to life.

By spending more time together and engaging in intentional, meaningful conversation, you'll be forming an organic connection that involves you and your husband giving one another your full attention. Due to all of the external forces of stimulation, devoting time to each other, as well as applying the lessons in communication learned from romance novels, expressing your emotions will become easier and more fulfilling.

While you can forge an emotional connection apart from physical intimacy, it should be noted that a healthy emotional connection will eventually lead to increased physical intimacy between you and your partner. The two go hand in hand, really, and the success of one can actually dictate the outcome of the other. That being said, this can only be accomplished when you remove the other emotional outlets in your marriage. By eliminating romance novels and any other medium used to substitute intimacy and a genuine emotional connection with your spouse, you'll be able to set realistic expectations in the marriage.

Alright: Now that you know what needs to be cut free from your marriage in order for it to thrive, we'll be moving on to the next chapter, which is going to tackle one of the greatest divides in the lives of modern women—career versus marriage. As you're most likely aware, women in our modern age are encouraged to expend all their efforts into their careers while neglecting their marriages and families. Let's take a closer look at how this common mistake is leading to unfulfillment and a faulty foundation in many, many marriages.

Chapter 6:
Pour Your Efforts Into Your House, Not Your Career

"And the Lord God said: 'It is not good that the man should be alone; I will make him a help meet for him.'" –Genesis 2:18, King James Bible Online, 1611e

As we start Chapter 6, let me bring to your mind an unfortunate truth: Our modern society has unleashed an arsenal of attacks against the family unit How has it done this? By targeting men and women with ideas and pursuits that seem harmless, but are deep down anything but. And as a result, we end up being pulled in multiple directions as we try to fulfill numerous roles in various facets of life. Our bosses want us to put in more hours at work, our families want us to spend more time with them, and our friends also want us to share more of our company with them as well.

But believe it or not, this issue affects women differently than men, as they are increasingly encouraged to pour more of their time and effort into their careers. And this begs the question: How can a woman, who is designed to be the administrator and organizer of the home, be expected to run a household, spend quality time with her spouse, effectively raise and train her children, and commit the remainder of her time to her career? As modern society continues to deem the roles of wife and mother as unnecessary burdens, while at the same time pushing a career-driven lifestyle on every woman, what is she really supposed to do?

Being a single, independent, and "liberated" woman is championed all throughout media and entertainment today—I'm sure you've noticed. As a matter of fact, many of the entertainers and musicians who look down on the traditional role of women in the household in favor of a career-focused lifestyle are committed wives and mothers themselves, aren't they? What they won't tell you, though, is that the time invested into one's family and household is not at all in vain.

As a woman, you are endowed with certain attributes that make you a natural homemaker, caregiver, and nurturer that men simply don't possess in the same capacity. And that is why the time and attention you give to your family is so invaluable; when done from a spirit of humility, love, respect, and care, it's an investment that will yield a much better quality of life for you and your family. Not only do you help to raise balanced and well-rounded children, but by truly embracing this role, you'll also be strengthening your marriage and reducing the risk of divorce.

As the scripture I opened this chapter with suggests, God made woman to be a "helpmeet" to a man, or a source of help that would be ideal for his life's purpose, which includes the building of a family to leave a lasting legacy. This was God's original design for the family.

Now, a woman's value should not be overshadowed, as a great deal of the functioning of a household is dependent on the multifaceted roles she plays in the family as a wife, leader, administrator, and—in many a household—a manager of family finances. But, of course, her role as a mother is of utmost importance to the security of the next generation. With that in mind, here is a list of some of the roles a woman must fulfill simultaneously in the household, on top of being expected to maintain a full-time career:

The Role of a Wife

A woman's role as the helpmeet to her husband is one of the most significant things she can accomplish in her life, apart from being a mother. Indeed, the role of a wife requires much more than modern society describes, which is yet another reason why marriages fail so often nowadays—there isn't enough understanding in the area of what being a wife *entails*. Most women go into marriages for selfish reasons, and when they don't perform the wifely duties required of them, their husbands are left dissatisfied, and the marriage begins to crumble.

Part of being a helpmeet to your husband includes sacrificing your personal pleasure and ambitions, setting a standard of morality in the family and in society, alleviating stress and tension from your husband, and being an agent of peace, stability, and order in the household. Without a doubt, creating an environment of peace and order is necessary for your husband to focus his energy on the economic provision of the family.

This is why as a wife, being able to control your emotions and your words is so important to his financial success. How can he focus on the economic upliftment of the family when he has to worry about chaos and drama at home? When you can encourage peace in the family and keep the home affairs in order, it creates the perfect balance that provides your husband with the clarity needed to generate wealth and financial security for you and your children. Think about it this way: Your ability to bring this level of emotional stability acts as the inspiration he needs to perform to his highest potential and achieve greatness in life.

In the same way that your husband invests his love in you, he looks to you to invest your love, sympathy, consolation, and understanding in him, in good and bad times. The true test of your character will be whether or not you can stand by him during hardship. When you can, it shows him that he can trust you enough to stand beside him when success comes.

The Role of Administrator of the Household

As previously mentioned, a woman acts as the administrator of the household, and this is why an orderly and disciplined home is essential to a healthy and productive family life. A woman's position in a family is like the role of a chief executive officer in a business. She is able to delegate tasks among family members according to their abilities and interests, ensuring that everyone gets involved in the daily rigmarole at home. This teaches young children responsibility at a young age and fosters inclusion in family matters.

Furthermore, the woman plays a significant part in the overall nutrition and well-being of the family by preparing and serving healthy meals, selecting and maintaining clothing, as well as furnishing and decorating the house. Have you ever heard someone say, "This place looks like it needs a woman's touch?" That's because a woman adds a certain sense of style and flavor to the interior aesthetic of a home, making it feel more like, well, a *home*.

Her administrative function also shines through when she plans a variety of social functions for the family, whether that be a birthday party, a movie night, or an adventurous family outing. This is done as a way to foster social development and build stronger bonds among the members of the family.

The Role of Manager of Family Income

So far, the first two roles we've discussed occupy quite a bit of time and energy, which makes it easier to understand why managing these family obligations along with a full-time career would be a struggle. But that isn't everything a wife is required to do. That's right—as alluded to earlier, she must also use her financial wisdom to manage the family income efficiently.

As a wife, you must be able to utilize the financial resources prudently when it comes to purchasing the necessities, comforts, and luxuries for the home. If you also work, whether within or outside the home, your earnings then also contribute to the overall income of the family.

However, it must be noted that one of the highest indicators of divorce rates and dissatisfaction in marriages is due to the wife outearning the husband. This can lead to disrespect, causing the wife to feel like she can survive without the husband's assistance, creating an atmosphere of competition. Now, of course, competing with your husband financially is one of the fastest ways to undermine his value as a man, and essentially tear apart your marriage.

Having a desire to outearn your husband is one of the main reasons why women tend to focus on their careers more than their marriage and family. Instead of trying to compete for the role of household breadwinner, it's better to let him focus on providing the money so that the two of you can work in unison in order to secure the best future for your marriage and family.

The Role of a Mother

As a woman, you are placed in the pivotal position of being one of the most influential people in your children's lives. Indeed, as the one who assumes the burden of childbearing, you play a defining role, which evolves into the responsibility of child-rearing as they grow older. Now, being the primary authority in child-rearing, you are responsible for cultivating the child's habits, cleanliness, orderliness, and industriousness. Not to mention it's your job to instill good morals and values in them.

This, of course, will all be accomplished through the personal contact you and the children share during their formative years, which will dictate their rate of development and behavioral patterns. In many ways, you're literally holding the future in your hands. Therefore, you will be held accountable for whether they are perceived as disciplined or unruly children.

Long before the children encounter a classroom, you will be the very first person they learn from. From you, they will learn to adopt attitudes, mannerisms, and special traits due to the prolonged time you spend together. Everything they learn from you, their mother, whether good or bad, will be used to shape their personalities.

Think of the amount of intentional care, time, effort, and cautious guidance that has to go into being a mother and raising a family. It's like a full-time job all by itself! If you do indeed have children, then you certainly know all the hats you have to wear—including that of the family nurse. Because of your intrinsically caring nature, you are also deeply concerned about the health and physical well-being of every member of the family, I'm positive.

Consider this: If you decide against placing your children in a daycare for the first few years, you'll be the sole source of their nutrition, hygiene, grooming, and also their first bonded human interaction outside of the womb. Let's not forget the sickly child who waiting in bed for you to take their temperature, or the adolescent who seeks your valuable advice about a school crush.

Your concern for your children's health and wellness also extends to the food you prepare them, ensuring it's tasty and nutritious. Then there's the ambiance of comfort and tranquility that you create indoors, using your talents to transform the home into an inviting and joyful environment. A woman living out her spousal and motherly roles makes her a matriarchal pillar in the family, after all.

If you have daughters, your role as a mother also sets an example for them on the type of women they should aspire to become. Your sons, of course, will benefit from your presence because it will teach them the good qualities to look for in a woman when choosing a wife. But your daughters, in particular, will be most influenced by you since they are more likely to model their entire lives as adult women after your example.

So, as you've read thus far, there is a lot of effort that goes into maintaining a family. And your service to your husband is fraught with spousal duties as is, and those duties only get multiplied when children are introduced. After all this is considered, the amount of sacrifice that must be made becomes fundamentally clear. Where, among duties to her husband, her children, and her home, can a woman possibly find time for a career? In the long run, you'll look back and realize that your prioritizing of family over career has been worth it. In fact, that's an understatement.

Now, when your children think of you, they won't be thinking of the priceless sacrifice you made for them by being a loving mother, home administrator, disciplinarian, teacher, organizer, and health officer. They'll see you as a provider, just like their father. This isn't meant to imply that all your husband does is provide resources and nothing else; he also offers emotional support, guidance, and discipline. But as a mother, the value you bring to the family is best expressed at home, and no amount of money can substitute that.

All this being said, being a mother doesn't mean that you can't contribute to the income of the family. In today's economic market, being able to contribute to your husband's provision allows you to save more, invest more, and secure your future and that of your children. Just exercise caution as you do so, of course.

See, the imbalance is created when you allocate more of your time to your career than you do to your family. Your husband will not be able to do the things you do as a mother. And if he is the breadwinner in the family, he also needs your support as a wife to keep him motivated to dominate in his respective field of business.

Balancing Work and Family

Speaking of balance, I'm now going to highlight some of the ways that'll allow you to effectively juggle work, home, and family demands within your marriage, according to Medium (Jamal, 2022). Remember, your marriage should not be put on the chopping block in exchange for your career, so learning to prioritize your husband and family is essential to your success as a wife and a mother. With that, see if these tips work for you:

Spending Quality Time Together

Between the demands of your job, career, or business, as well as tending to household responsibilities, setting aside quality time to spend with your husband can seem like an afterthought. But failing to prioritize this part of your life can put your marriage in a vulnerable position. Remember what I said earlier about making investments in your marriage? Well, think of spending quality time with your husband as one of those investments, and the return on that investment is a long and healthy marriage.

Try to make it a tradition to schedule regular date nights and spend weekends alone enjoying each other's company You can take these occasions to catch up on your personal lives. Turn off your phone—and cut off all social media, for that matter—and if you have children, organize for them to spend the weekend at a trusted relative's house. As we discussed in Chapter 3, your relationship with your husband predates your obligations to your children and will outlive them once they've left the nest. So, prioritize these date nights and special weekends.

Designing a Family Calendar

You want everyone in the family to be on one accord when it comes to any upcoming events, vacations, and chores that need to be done. Why? Because this way, you allow for the preparation of everyone involved and as such, they can make time to balance work and family. When everyone in the family knows what is expected of them—and when it's expected—it helps to alleviate the stress of poorly-timed decisions. A family calendar ensures that everyone equally shares their time between work and family.

Sharing the Responsibilities

Balancing the responsibilities of work, marriage, and parenthood can take its toll on the best of us. So, in order to reduce the stress and pressure that comes with being a working parent, sharing the responsibilities between you and your husband is the only viable option. Similarly to creating a family calendar, you can create a schedule that divides the responsibilities between you and your husband based on your abilities and work schedule.

For example, childcare would be your forte, especially if it's a newborn baby that requires a lot of your care, attention, and coddling. Other responsibilities like household chores and outdoor errands could be covered by your husband during this time, for instance, since you'll mostly be preoccupied with the baby.

Taking Time for Yourself (Self-Love)

Mark 10:8 reads, "And they twain shall be one flesh: so then they are no more twain, but one flesh" (King James Bible Online, 1611f). As such, your marriage union has indeed made you and your husband one flesh. However, while this remains true, each of you still requires a bit of personal space now and again. After all, you won't be able to truly love anyone else in your family unless you first love yourself. And so, setting aside time for self-reflection and self-care is key to finding balance in your work and family life.

You can start by devoting a set amount of time each day to doing something you truly enjoy, like reading, writing, exercising, swimming, or simply taking a walk. Doing this will give you a break from your daily routine and help create the balance needed to continue with your daily tasks.

Openly Discussing Your Future Goals as a Couple

As a married couple, it's important to have frequent check-ins, as these give you the platform to openly talk about the forward movement of your relationship and family. You and your husband communicating about work and home issues is key to knowing what direction you're moving in and whether or not you're meeting the goals you've set for yourselves. It's also a way of ensuring that everyone is on the same page and that their mental, emotional, and physical health is in check.

Finding Balance by Setting Boundaries

Setting boundaries between work and family is another constructive way of balancing your work and family life responsibilities. Essentially, this entails the nonnegotiable limits you and your partner agree upon for the amount of time each of you spends at work and how much time is spent with family. This is a great way of keeping each other in check, as it ensures that neither one of you is neglecting what is most important, thus maintaining balance in the marriage.

Time together as a family is important, and so you can do this by selecting specific days and times detailing when each partner is expected to be spending time at home with family and when they're expected to be at work.

Being Willing and Flexible

You may have scheduled your entire week in advance, but then life threw one of its inevitable curveballs, and boom, your careful planning was for naught. Planning is necessary when trying to balance work and family life, but we can't always plan for life's unpredictability. That's why being flexible is an important part of the process. As such, both you and your partner should be willing to adjust your plans when necessary. Being flexible in your work and home schedule can create a more balanced life as you do your best to take into account any unforeseen circumstances.

Whether you and your husband are newlyweds or have just begun to grow your family, being able to balance your professional and family lives will help to even the amount of stress either one of you has to endure. Of course, your jobs may be different in terms of the physical and mental effort required from you, but it's not impossible to find a way that works best for your unique situation.

Strengthening the Team Dynamic

There's an African proverb that says, "If you want to go fast, go alone. If you want to go far, go together" (COPH Staff, 2016). While this saying can be applied to various aspects of life, it best applies to the context of marriage and the idea of teamwork that should exist between you and your spouse. When you're building a team with someone, even if it's a two-man unit, there's a certain degree of compromise that is required from both parties.

For example, you may be expected to accommodate some of your partner's likes, dislikes, and lifestyle habits. And, likewise, you're probably expecting them to accommodate some of yours as well. Surely, certain adjustments will be required as you transition from single life to married life, but this is what it takes to build a strong foundation for marriage that will stand firm against life's storms.

Marriage.com has listed a few principles that should be introduced into a marriage from the very beginning as a means of nurturing your marital relationship and, as a result, strengthening it as well (Pace, 2020). As with any solid structure that stands the test of time, the foundation is the most important stage in the building process. But even if you've been married for years and you're not pleased with the direction your marriage is going, here are some of the things you can do to improve the relationship with your husband and rebuild a stronger, sturdier foundation:

1. **Commit to your spouse.**

    Unfortunately, commitment in a monogamous marriage is not favored in today's society. Indeed, the world seems to lean more toward satisfying the pleasures of the flesh and exploring less conservative types of relationships. But if you're looking for safety, security, and openness in your relationship, then commitment is one of the principles that you'll need to establish in your marriage.

Commitment in marriage is something that calls for you to make your partner your other half on this journey, and for them to reciprocate that sentiment. But this is not a light confession, and is, in fact, exactly what makes this type of marriage a solid, lasting union.

Announcing your commitment to your spouse is a testament to your loyalty, faithfulness, and consistency to them, and is meant to mirror your commitment to God. Part of being committed is being able to show up as the person your spouse needs you to be on any given day. But what does that mean, you ask? Well, it goes back to knowing and understanding your spouse on a profound, emotional level.

For example, if you can sense that your spouse is stressed, and he communicates their insecurity to you, that lets you know that you need to be the strong one on that day or during that period. Likewise, if you're the one who's feeling needy and requires your husband's emotional support, after communicating this to him, he should follow up by giving you what you need in that moment.

Essentially, you want to be certain that you can rely on your spouse to keep his word when he professes his faithfulness, love, and devotion to you. Likewise, he also wants that to be reciprocated. So, when you say your vows, "For richer or for poorer, for better or for worse, until death do us part," that's a commitment that you made to your spouse that he's expecting you to follow through with.

2. Communication is key.

Now, you've heard it being echoed throughout the book, but here it is again—*communication is key*! There's a valid reason for this, though. Communication, especially in a long-term romantic relationship like a marriage, is directly related to the happiness and prosperity of that relationship.

Are you speaking your husband's language? As you know, communication is composed of more than just words—it involves nonverbal cues, body language, eye contact, and tone of voice, to name a few.

So, truly understanding the love language of your spouse may take some time because relationship communication skills don't come easily for everyone. It may take a few years for you to hone this skill, even, but don't worry: It gets easier as the years go by. Indeed, over time, you and your spouse will be able to comprehend each other's love languages and communicate more effectively.

3. Be intimate.

Intimacy exceeds the physical experience you and your husband share in the bedroom. True intimacy is a by-product of commitment that has been tried and proven. Being comfortable with sharing the most profound and vulnerable parts of yourself with your partner is true intimacy. This includes being open to sharing your deepest fears, greatest hopes, dearest dreams, and most personal pains. You have to be willing to share the most sensitive bits of information about yourself with your spouse, which may include childhood traumas and unhealed experiences.

This level of vulnerability is exactly what true intimacy is because it can actually be used to strengthen a marriage and keep it exciting. Intimacy builds love and trust in a relationship, and that is precisely what makes it fulfilling. In the absence of intimacy, your marriage could quickly become a mundane chore, seeming more like a routine than a satisfying experience.

4. Practice patience.

If there are two things in life that will teach you patience, it's being in a marriage and raising children, because both of these will trigger you to become frustrated and react in anger. But herein is where you must exercise restraint and avoid acting on your emotions.

There are times when your husband will say something or respond to you in a way that prompts an illogical, emotional response from you. But when you exercise patience in your marriage, it leaves room for this very virtue to flourish. Indeed, with patience, you learn to let go of the things you can't control that are outside of yourself, and manage the things that are within your control (like your emotional responses).

This verse of scripture in Proverbs 15:1 is a perfect example of why patience should be exercised in your marriage: "A soft answer turneth away wrath: but grievous words stir up anger" (King James Bible Online, 1611h).

When you practice patience with your husband and your children, you learn to listen to understand, and not merely to respond. Being patient and slow to anger also creates an environment of peace, stability, and contentment in the family.

With these core marriage principles in place, your marriage will be able to stand the test of time against the many obstacles you'll face together. And although marriage in today's world has been bastardized due to the surplus of celebrity divorces being broadcast on TV and social media, it can be a rewarding experience for those who build a strong foundation using the principles listed above. And even if your marital foundation didn't start strong, there are still ways of strengthening your marriage from here on out.

Teamwork Makes the Marriage Work

1. Choose collaboration over competition.

With everyone else running the rat race of life and competing to reach the "finish line" before the other, the one place you don't want to feel like you're in a competition is in your own marriage, right? Therefore, you shouldn't be trying to compete with your husband to see who earns more or who is better at handling difficult situations. You should complement each other as a unit and work together using your individual strengths to build the best possible life for your family.

2. Get rid of outside "toxic" relationships.

Toxic relationships are often defined as ones wherein a person demonstrates behaviors that make you feel unhappy, disrespected, and dominated, and are filled with deceit and a lack of support, to boot. But, honestly, a better definition of a toxic relationship is a relationship that demands more than it gives. Relationships that fit this mold can include family members, friends, coworkers, or any others you and your husband deal with frequently. If you find that these relationships are taking more of your time, energy, resources, and peace while not giving back any in return, it may be time to cut your losses as they are no longer beneficial to you or your marriage.

3. Surprise your spouse with kind gestures.

If you're honest with yourself, you probably love it when your husband spoils you with dinner reservations at your favorite restaurants or with a bouquet of your favorite flowers. He does these things because he wants to show you that he cares and thinks about you all the time. So, how do you think he'll feel if you do the same for him?

Well, in order to reciprocate his kind gestures and invest in strengthening your marriage, consider inviting your husband out to the movies to watch a new action movie, even though you might prefer a romantic comedy! You could also surprise him by cooking his favorite meal or baking his favorite dessert.

4. Encourage your spouse regularly.

Part of maintaining a strong marriage involves your spouse feeling good about himself. No one wants to be around someone who constantly looks down on them or makes their efforts feel overlooked, after all. And so, to keep your husband feeling like the great catch he is, remind him of his importance to you and how much of a positive influence he is in your life. Tell him that you appreciate all he's been doing—both overtly and behind the scenes—to make your lives easier. This is more than just an ego boost; it's a way of letting him know that you see and understand the value he brings into your life and, as such, you're grateful for every moment of it.

5. Consider adopting a pet.

Provided your husband (or yourself, obviously) actually likes animals, you can suggest adopting a kitten or a puppy. Pets are known for bringing a sense of joy to a home, and the collaborative effort between you and your spouse in taking care of the animal can even strengthen your union.

6. Make plans that both of you can enjoy.

You and your partner were individuals before you got married, and so you might have adopted different hobbies prior to your union. To this day, your husband may prefer a day at the beach while you may prefer a day at the spa.

With this contrast in mind, rather than making plans that only involve activities you enjoy, try finding out what your spouse enjoys doing and try to participate in some of those activities. You might just end up liking them! But even if you don't, your husband will appreciate your selflessness and do the same for you in return.

7. Keep your bedroom activity interesting.

While the emotional connection holds a lot of weight in forming your marriage bond, a thriving sex life is the ultimate key to the success of any marriage. Make no mistake, physical attraction and sexual satisfaction are two defining factors that add to the "enjoyable" aspect of a marriage.

But as wonderful as sex may be, you need to spice things up in the bedroom every now and then, as otherwise, it becomes rigid. To keep your sex life hot and active, consider visiting your local adult shop for an enticing bedroom outfit, or shopping online for some seductive lingerie. Seduction plays a huge part in sexual attraction, so you want to make sure that you're doing your best to seduce your husband.

8. Don't sweat the small stuff.

It can seem comical at times how two adults who are in love can end up bickering and arguing about trivial matters. There will always be a never-ending supply of insignificant problems that arise in your marriage, but it's not a good habit to start an argument with your husband when they do.

In most cases, stressing over small matters in a relationship usually stems from either partner's obsession with those unimportant issues. So, you should examine yourself to see if you are the cause of the bickering because of your fixation on minor problems. When done excessively, it can be seen as a form of criticism, and your husband will soon come to loathe your company.

9. Reminisce on life together.

Have you ever sat with your husband and backtracked on your life together, in utter awe of how far your journey has come? Reminiscing together is a way of reconnecting your relationship when it feels ever so slightly detached. In particular, reminding each other of why you fell in love can rejuvenate your emotional attachment in a truly lasting way.

10. Be responsible for your actions.

Let's be real here for a moment: Marriages are between two adults, right? And as adults, you both need to be responsible for your actions. Your husband shouldn't have to be in a position where he constantly feels sorry for you, and neither should you. Rather, try to take accountability, acknowledge your faults, and ask your partner for help whenever you're faced with a problem.

11. Leave the past behind.

As the saying goes, "The only time you should ever look back is to see how far you've come." It's counterproductive to constantly bring up situations from your husband's past that happened years ago. Take a look at what is happening around you in the present moment, and where you are aiming to go in the future.

In every marriage, forgiveness is vital, because you are both imperfect people who make mistakes. If you want your union to be strengthened, don't put so much weight on the days of old, but rather, focus on the present and look toward the forward in anticipation.

12. Engage in "sex talk."

Conversations about sex should not be taboo with your husband. By now, you should know your spouse well enough in the bedroom to have open discussions about it, such as your sexual patterns, likes and dislikes during sex, personal fantasies, and so on. The more open and comfortable you are about having these sex-topic discussions as a couple, the more joy and relationship satisfaction you'll experience.

13. Learn conflict-resolution skills.

Because conflict and misunderstandings are common in a marriage, learning to manage them by compromising, coming up with agreeable solutions, or agreeing to disagree, are all ways of avoiding a large-scale conflict.

And, naturally, the more conflicts you resolve as a couple, the stronger your marriage will become. If you already have children, it's also important for them to see you and your spouse handling conflict in a healthy and productive manner.

With all that has been said in this chapter, let me reinstate its main lesson: You should learn to put your marriage ahead of your career. There are so many women today who have fallen into the trap of feminism ideology, which encourages them to chase their careers and financial security, only to accomplish those things and end up lonely, single, and childless.

Regardless of how modern society tries to repackage women, they are intrinsically made to be nurturers of themselves, their husbands, and their children. No amount of professional success can fill the void of a natural, feminine woman. She will always feel unfulfilled from being out of alignment with one of her greatest callings in life, which is to be a wife and a mother.

Moving on, in Chapter 7, we'll be covering how you can overcome the need for perfectionism in your life before allowing an intimate marital connection with your husband.

Chapter 7:

Don't Worry About Imperfections in Your Life Getting in the Way of Having Time for Your Husband

The saying "foreplay begins in the kitchen" holds a lot of truth. And I believe it applies especially well to long-term relationships and marriages. If you're hearing this phrase for the first time while reading this, basically, it means that foreplay—and the build-up to sex in general—doesn't just begin behind closed bedroom doors, and trust me: There's a lot of value to this insight.

As a quick aside, this phrase applies mostly to men, as they are the main instigators of foreplay. As such, this would be great advice for your husband if he's trying to reignite that honeymoon passion later on in the marriage. However, what we're going to be centering on in this chapter is the tendency of some wives to want everything in their environment to be tidied up and completed before tending to their husband's sexual needs. This could be the dishes, the laundry, or general house cleaning—the point is it can all be a distraction, and none of it should ever take priority when it comes to satisfying your spouse.

I actually encourage husbands to make time to assist their wives with home chores and child responsibilities so that she doesn't feel overwhelmed. And, of course, as a result of this assistance, these wives are put in a more relaxed state of mind. That being said, your marriage can quickly enter the danger zone when you adopt an attitude of "sex can wait until..."—until what? Until other household priorities are taken care of first. The thing is, if your husband is willing to assist you with the work at home, then you should prioritize his sexual needs above needing to tend to household duties.

First off, try to empathize with your husband and see how his mind processes your words when you say, "I'm not in the mood and can't be present in the moment if the laundry isn't done and the dishes aren't washed." In your mind, you're thinking that the work at home should come first because the home tasks are more or less your domain. What your husband hears is that his sexual needs are lower on the priority list when compared to washing the dishes and mopping the floor.

You might even genuinely believe that completing your house chores should come first. But, unquestionably, one of the primary reasons your husband married you was for sex, and so without argument, it ranks much higher on his list of priorities—especially if he's a hardworking man who relishes his spare time with you. Withholding sex to accomplish other tasks or using sex as a bargaining tool to get what you want is also ineffective, and can lead to greater problems down the road.

As a woman, you should be aware of the fact that men have a much higher sex drive than their female counterparts, and therefore sex is much higher on his list of priorities. And if you also place meeting those sexual needs high on your priority list, then his love for you will be endless. On that note, I'll remind you here that the enemy hates Christian marriages, and if he can find an opening into your union through offense or the temptation of adultery, he will capitalize on it. You should be delighted to know that your husband directs such a high level of sexual interest toward you, and as such, you should reciprocate that level of interest so that your marriage union remains strong.

In addition to willingly submitting to his sexual requests, Family Life highlights a few other words, attitudes, and actions that you should discontinue if you would like to improve your marriage—or simply want it to last (Starcher, 2018). Here are a few of these helpful suggestions:

Stop Thinking That You Always Know Best

I've heard women try to ridicule men by saying things like, "Without a woman in the house, men are like helpless little children." This way of thinking stems from the knowledge that they are better at managing a home because of their inherent qualities. But it doesn't mean that if a man does something differently, it's automatically wrong. For some women, the belief that they are better skilled at keeping a home can lead them to believe that they're always right and that a man's suggestions lack value or are plainly wrong. But a woman's need to be "right" in every situation is nothing more than a constant need to be in control.

Your Husband Isn't One of Your Girlfriends

Men and women are different in more than just their physical appearance. They also process information and react to life situations differently. For example, you may have heard it said that men aren't "big talkers." Unlike women, they don't easily communicate their thoughts and emotions through conversation. Understanding this, you should avoid talking your husband's ear off, figuratively speaking, with endless detailed conversations about things you would normally discuss with your friends—things he doesn't really care about. Reserve the girl talk for your girlfriends.

Don't Prioritize Others Above Your Husband

God's intent for man and woman to become one under the covenant of marriage was so that husband and wife could meet each other's need for closeness and intimacy in a human relationship. That's the reason why he created Eve out of Adam's rib, as it says in Genesis 2:18, "It is not good that man should be alone; I will make for him an help meet for him."

But God goes further in Genesis 2:24, stating, "Therefore shall a man leave his mother and father, and shall cleave unto his wife: and they shall be one flesh." This scripture clearly explains that, once you are joined unto your husband and you become one flesh, your mother, father, siblings, friends, and even children should come after your husband. Therefore, putting anyone before your husband can cause him to feel like he has taken second place in your heart, leading him to withdraw emotionally.

Don't Use Sex as a Bargaining Tool With Your Husband

As a woman, you understand that one of your husband's main desires from you is physical intimacy in the form of sex. This should be a natural expectation that you should be excited to share with him. However, there are some women who, whether intentionally or unintentionally, use sex as a bargaining tool to get what they want.

For example, they may say, "After you help me fold this mountain of clothes, I'll give you what you want." Meeting your husband's sexual needs should not be up for negotiation, though, because 1 Corinthians 7:4 tells us, "The wife hath not power over her own body, but the husband: and likewise the husband hath not power over his own body, but the wife" (King James Bible Online, 1611a). Therefore, if you use sex as a negotiation tool, you should discontinue this practice as you are not submitting to your husband.

Don't Dishonor Your Husband

To dishonor someone means to give them little to no weight or value. So, in the context of marriage, what are some of the ways in which you may be dishonoring your husband? For one, constantly complaining to him when you're aware that it's frustrating him—especially in front of others—is a surefire way of dishonoring him. Also, correcting your husband in front of others or even cutting him off mid-sentence under the guise of finishing his sentences may communicate the message to him and to others, "What you have to say is irrelevant," or "You don't know what you're saying so I'll finish your sentence for you."

Don't Cause Your Husband to Be Defensive

Your husband wants to know that you have his back and that he's not looking foolish in front of you. If you notice something he's doing is wrong or that he's made a mistake, don't call him out on it when you see him putting in the effort. For example, if you've been complaining about the leak in the bathroom sink, and he said he's fixed it for the sixth time—but it's *still* leaking—don't tell him that he has no idea what he's doing and should stop trying. This will likely only make the situation worse.

Instead of responding impulsively, carefully consider your words before speaking. Ask yourself, "Will my words be helpful or cause more harm? Would I be encouraging him with my response?" Sometimes, it's better to remain quiet before responding. Proverbs 10:19 says, "In the multitude of words, there wanteth not sin: but he that refraineth his lips is wise" (King James Bible Online, 1611k).

Don't Make Your Husband Earn Your Respect

As I stated briefly before, respect is a man's native tongue and shouldn't have to be something he earns from you. Many women believe that she'll only respect her husband when he *earns* her respect. That mentality is a recipe for marriage disaster because not respecting your husband will cause him to shut down emotionally.

Demanding your husband to do things in order to gain sexual satisfaction is also a way of making him earn your respect. You should respect him enough to meet his sexual needs without the need for manipulation. Keep Ephesians 5:33 in mind, which says: "Nevertheless let every one of you in particular so love his wife even as himself; and the wife see that she reverence her husband" (King James Bible Online, 1611d).

Stop Taking the Lead for Your Husband

Many women get impatient with their husbands when they believe they're not taking the lead or taking action quickly enough. You may see what needs to be done and think that your husband is slow to take charge, and as such, you may begin to do it *for* him. Perhaps your impatience is causing you to jump the gun when in reality, all you need to do is wait on your husband's leadership.

Avoid Self-Help Books and Relationship Gurus

When it comes to marriage problems, above any other remedy, your first line of defense is the Word of God. It has everything you need to remedy the obstacles you may face along your marriage journey, and so that's where you should be searching for answers. 2 Peter 1:3 reminds us that we have all we need for life: "According as his divine power has given unto us all things that pertain unto life and godliness, through the knowledge of him that hath called us to glory and virtue" (King James Bible Online, 1611c).

Now, the takeaway from this section has been to underline the fact that your husband's sexual needs should be prioritized above any other household responsibility. Moving on, we'll be going over a few strategies for devoting time to your husband.

Make Connection and Intimacy a Priority

As a married couple with children, life can seem like a runaway freight train with no brakes—and more literally, it can seem like life doesn't give you a break. But if you value your marriage and want the intimacy to last, you have to *create* those breaks. The grass is only green where you take the time to water it, so by making time for your husband amid the busyness of life, you can keep the lifeline of your marriage pulsating.

On that note, here are some of the approaches you can take to secure more time with your husband:

- **Give the kids a bedtime:** You and your husband enforce the rules at home, and therefore a set bedtime should be instituted for your children, regardless of their ages. Both young and older children are required to get sufficient sleep so that their brains and bodies can function to their maximum potential. But besides a set bedtime being good for the children's well-being, it's also a way to give you and your husband quality time together—whether that be talking, watching a movie or TV show, or making love.

- **Communicate often:** Take advantage of the technological age we live in by keeping the lines of communication open with your spouse through texts, direct messages, phone calls, and voice notes. Remember, *foreplay begins in the kitchen*, so sending sexually seductive texts, thank-you texts, and flirtatious texts throughout the day is a simple way of maintaining communication. Then, when you get home, keep the communication going by conversing while cooking dinner, followed by before you go to bed, and then when you wake up.

- **Give him the best of everything:** Making time for your husband can also be expressed through your intention and the amount of effort you put into doing simple things for him. Consider: When you're cooking a meal, do you go above and beyond to make it spectacular? Does he get the best cut of meat at the table? Do you give him your brightest smiles in the morning and the best kisses before he goes to work? Does he get your undivided attention when you spend time together, even above your children, social media, other family members, and your career?

- **Go on spontaneous getaways without the kids:** Once children enter the picture, it's easy to revolve your lives around them. But you also need time to relax together with your hubby—without the kids. Even if it's for one night, you can lodge at a campsite with a beautiful view, book a hotel resort in the off-season, or rent an Airbnb for the weekend. And these getaways don't always have to be for a birthday or anniversary celebration—make it a spontaneous retreat just to celebrate love and life!

- **Have a regular date night:** I know how difficult it can be to find time to go out for dinner when you have children. Sometimes the babysitter isn't available and there are no relatives who live close by who can watch them while you go out. In that case, consider swapping babysitting with a friend who also has kids at least twice a month. Those times that you can't go out, plan a romantic dinner at home with your husband while the kids are sleeping or enjoying a movie night.

- **Be accountable to each other:** Besides being obvious lovers in your marriage, you and your husband are also supposed to be each other's best friends and biggest supporters. And true friends hold each other accountable and want each other to be the best version of themselves.

We can see the value of having friendship and accountability in marriage in Ecclesiastes 4:9-10, which reads, "Two are better than one; because they have a good reward for their labor. For if they fall, the one will lift up his fellow" (King James Bible Online, 1611e).

If you're having trouble in a particular area, ask your husband to keep you accountable. For example, if you're on a weight-loss diet but tend to resort to junk food whenever you're stressed, you can ask your husband to remove all the junk food from the house and replace it with healthier options. Or he can remind you of your fitness goals so that you're motivated to stay on track with your diet.

Your accountability to each other takes one-on-one time—be it evaluating a shopping list, coming up with alternatives, or scheduling a meal prep for the week. You can also find ways to be accountable to your partner too, because you're both fallible in some way and may need the extra guidance and motivation at times.

- **Couples who pray together stay together:** Praying and worshiping together is one of the best ways to spend time with your spouse because this is where you truly become one in soul and spirit. Praying together with your husband unlocks a level of intimacy that knits your hearts in oneness together with Christ, fulfilling the scripture of "two becoming one flesh." Also, the scripture verse in Ecclesiastes 4:12 which says, "...a threefold cord is not easily broken," also alludes to the strength of a marriage that makes God the center of it.

   Praying together on one accord also guarantees that your prayers are heard and answered by God. To keep track of God's faithfulness to you, start by writing down the times he has answered your prayers in a notebook. And every so often during the year, you can review the book with your husband and spend time simply thanking God for His grace, mercy, and faithfulness over the years.

No matter how often the external forces of life (job, career, business, children, ministry, etc.) try to create obstacles to keep you and your spouse divided, never neglect the importance of prioritizing your marriage. Marriage is a ministry in itself that represents God's relationship with the body of believers, so

118

prioritizing yours in spite of all the pressures that surround you makes for a genuine expression of God's love for us.

Now that we've gone over some strategies for making time for your husband while dealing with the challenges of life, we'll now be delving into the importance of setting time aside as a couple, while going over some specific ways of doing so.

Fostering Intimate Moments

Previously, we expounded on some of the ways to prioritize the physical and emotional intimacy in your marriage, and a lot of what was mentioned pointed toward regular date nights, weekend getaways, and other common ways to spend together. But what if I told you that there were other—often more underrated ways—of prioritizing your marriage? Here are some of the simple yet powerful ways you might be neglecting:

1. **Create boundaries.**

   In the same way you create boundaries as an individual because of the need to preserve your energy, peace of mind, emotional well-being, and resources, you also need to set boundaries in your marriage for many of those same reasons.

   Setting boundaries from external factors protects the equilibrium of your marital relationship from things or people who may be harmful to the harmony and balance you've created. You'd be surprised how certain people may come into your life disguised as family or friends, pretending to want to spend time with you just to cause a separation in your marriage.

   Being mindful enough to manage the activities and people you expend your energy on is key to ensuring that you conserve the best of that energy for your spouse. You'll also want to establish boundaries that protect the privacy of your relationship by making parts of your marriage off-limits to the public.

When it comes to anything or anyone that threatens the peace and stability of your marriage, you should opt for a no-tolerance policy. Why? Because when the health of your marriage is compromised, everything else attached to it will be compromised too.

2. **Consult one another before making decisions.**

The moment you get married, everything about your life changes. While before you were used to doing things alone—living alone, shopping alone, eating alone, spending time alone—all that changes when you decide to become one with your spouse. And as such, the choices you make now will not only affect you but your partner also—whether directly or indirectly.

Of course, you should use your discretion here, as smaller decisions won't always require your partner's input. But bigger decisions—the ones that will undeniably affect both of your lives—should be decided upon together. Since you are a joint unit with your spouse, consulting him for his perspective is a great way of showing consideration and respect. If there is a disagreement or difference in perspective, at least it gives you both a chance to talk things over and realign yourselves before making a final decision.

3. **Set specific goals together.**

Another aspect of your marriage that involves joint decision-making and planning is setting specific goals together. Similarly to the previous point, when you were single, you might've had specific goals that you wanted to accomplish for whatever reason.

Well, in a marriage, you now need to share relationship goals with your husband, as you both decide upon the direction in which you want the relationship to go. Indeed, sharing relationship goals with your partner is transformative because it requires you to prioritize your spouse, and furthermore, it makes you hold each other accountable.

According to Overcomers Counseling, creating short-term goals is healthy for your marriage because it opens the door for both partners to talk about their desires (Ayeni-Bepo, 2023). Some of your short-term relationship goals may include the following:

- separating family time from work time
- committing to weekly romantic dates
- planning monthly outdoor family activities
- cooking dinner together
- going to the beach every Sunday
- taking a weekend trip abroad as a couple every year

You can also set long-term goals together, which is obviously a much bigger commitment. Some long-term goals, however, could include one of these:

- saving to buy a house or a car
- saving for your children's college tuition
- investing in the health of your family

Long-term goals, in particular, encourage a sense of commitment and trust in both you and your husband because you're both pursuing something that benefits many more lives than just your own. Focusing on reaching financial goals together is also a way of exploring the strengths and weaknesses of one another. For example, you'll be exposed to each other's spending habits, food preferences, household habits, and overall money management habits.

4. Be direct when addressing problems.

How you address conflict in your marriage says a lot about how much you prioritize your relationship. Problems are bound to arise in even the healthiest of marriages because we are all imperfect people, but dealing with those problems can sometimes seem uncomfortable and cumbersome. This is especially true when anyone has to admit responsibility for being triggered or reacting irrationally.

It takes a lot of vulnerability and emotional maturity to admit to a fault, but both partners may not be on the same level of maturity. And so, what happens is that most of the problems get swept under the rug because that feels like the easiest choice. But easier isn't always more convenient, and before long, those unresolved issues will rise to the surface once more and begin to negatively affect the relationship.

The more difficult but ultimately fulfilling option would be to address the problem head-on and come to a healthy resolution. Not only does this teach you not to allow problems to linger in your marriage, but it also leads to you feeling more connected as a couple. By working together to overcome your marital conflicts promptly, you're essentially prioritizing the future of your marriage.

5. **Choose your words wisely.**

Being married to your husband implies being extremely close to him—closer than anyone else in your life. Such closeness makes both of you vulnerable to each other's words, which is why you should prioritize your spouse's feelings by carefully choosing what you say.

I mentioned earlier that besides perhaps his mother, you're most likely the woman in his life he can communicate his feelings to most openly. And the way you respond to him speaks volumes, so learn to validate what he feels and not be judgmental, or worse—dismissive.

In particular, try to empathize with the fact that he probably hasn't had much experience communicating his feelings. With that in mind, listen to him to the best of your ability, and be emotionally supportive of him. Also, respond thoughtfully to what he says, even if it may come across as childish to you.

Not every day will be great, and you may be going through your own stresses, but be wary of responding in anger or transferring your frustration from outside pressures onto him. As well, try not to let a bad day damage the emotional connection you have with your husband.

Also, be sure to speak words of reassurance and encouragement to him, reminding him of how much he means to you. Compliment him every now and then on not just his appearance, but also his work ethic or thoughtfulness toward you and your children.

And that just about does it for Chapter 7. We've covered some valuable wisdom in regard to prioritizing your husband's sexual and emotional needs. By applying these strategies to your marriage, you will be demonstrating the utmost respect to your husband—and turning things around for the better.

Alright, we'll now be heading into another area of showing respect in your marriage in Chapter 8, which is through the use of body language. Intrigued? Let's keep going.

Chapter 8:

Use Your Body Language to Show Respect

At the onset of this chapter, let me just offer up a quick reminder: I have been writing this book under the assumption that it is being read by a wife who not only wants to show respect to her husband but is also actively looking for ways to do so. God commanded for you to respect your husband, but I am by no means implying that because of what God said in His Word, you are therefore required to do each and every thing suggested in this book. My job here is simply to explore some of the ways in which you can show respect to your husband if, of course, it is your desire to do so.

There are multiple ways in which you can respect and show respect to your husband. We've already covered some superb ones, as you know. But again, every way that I list won't apply to everyone. You need to evaluate yourself and be honest with the type of wife you are to see which points will be truly useful to you.

Now, keeping all this in mind, I also want you to consider this as we dive into the content of this chapter: In no way are the following meant to demean you, or any women for that matter. Think of them as tools for your marriage tool kit—they're available for you to use on your own terms.

I've said in previous chapters that respect is the language of men. But what's more is that respect, particularly among men, is inherently hierarchical—sort of like a chain of command. Basically, when you show someone respect, you're acknowledging the fact that they are higher up in the hierarchy. So, you can do this by showing someone how high up they are, but you can also convey respect by showing them that they're *higher in rank* than someone else who they think is high up in the chain.

Okay, so you'll probably recall the counterpart to the central argument of this book, which is that while women struggle to show respect to their husbands, men struggle to show love to their wives. And this follows then, that most men—even those with marital problems—find it easier to show respect to their wives than to show them love. Why? Because again, respect is simply the language of men. So, for this next section on showing respect with your body language, the main idea is that a wife can elevate her husband by demonstrating hierarchical deference all through what she does with her body.

Surely, you're familiar with the phrase "actions speak louder than words." This is an accurate statement because things like body language, eye contact, and other gestures can make someone feel respected and validated before you even open your mouth to speak.

Nonverbal communication can be used in various settings to convey respect, such as business and casual atmospheres, but we're going to be talking about how you can use this form of communication to—once more—show respect to your husband. According to Khyati Gupta Babbar in her LinkedIn article, these are some of the ways you can use your body language to establish rapport or to seem engaged. Consider applying these to your marriage:

Giving Your Best Attention

To show that your listener has your undivided attention, you'll want to use what is called the "fronting method." Fronting is done by aligning your head, torso, and toes toward the person you're talking to. By fronting someone, you're communicating a level of nonverbal respect to them, letting them know that they have your full attention. While this is commonly done in a professional setting, like with an employer or a potential client, you can also try this with your husband the next time you're engaged in conversation.

It's All in the Eyes

You may have heard the saying, "The eyes are the windows to the soul." What this simply means is that a lot can be discovered about a person's emotions and interests by the way they communicate with their eyes. So, whenever you're engaged in conversation with your husband, maintain eye contact for 60–70% of the conversation. This is usually a natural occurrence when speaking with someone you have a genuine interest in. However, some people are shyer than others, so it can be difficult for them to maintain eye contact with the one they love.

Maintaining this level of eye contact with your husband is important because anything less will signal to him that you may not be that interested in him or that the conversation is boring. However, anything more than 60-70% can also come across as awkward or even creepy.

Using Your Body Language to Show That You're Listening

Have you ever spoken to someone who said they were listening to you, but you still had to ask them, "Are you sure you're listening?" because their body language was saying something else? That's why, when someone's speaking, it's important to show them you're invested in the conversation. And you can do this by moving your torso forward a little, and even tilting your head a bit to the side to emphasize your ear. Doing this communicates to your husband that you're genuinely listening to what he's saying, which is a huge sign of respect.

Using Trust to Deepen the Bond

The power of touch can be used to help build trust in business relationships, such as through a handshake. But in your marriage, touching your husband can be seen as a way to build intimacy and deepen your bond. The higher up on the arm you go, the more intimate the touch comes across. And so, a touch on the shoulder, the torso, or the face can communicate your love, adoration, and respect for him. Just a slight pat on the arm or a gentle caress releases oxytocin, also known as the "love hormone," leading to an increased bond with your husband.

Nonverbal Communication in Marriage

The need for respect—and its expression—will always be different in the covenant of a marriage than in a business setting. One of the reasons for this is that respect for your husband is a command given to wives by God. The truth is that, since the Fall of Adam and Eve, women have been implanted with the seed of rebellion toward their husbands and a desire to dominate them.

Therefore, conflict will always arise in marriages, and this is due to the fallen nature of the woman. And it's because of this fallen nature that God specifically gave respect for your husband as a command in Ephesians 5:33: "Nevertheless let every one of you in particular so love his wife even as himself;

and the wife see that she reverence her husband." "Reverence" here, of course, means respect.

Now that we know what lies at the core of a woman's capacity for disrespecting her husband, here are some tips from Radiant Marriage on how to actively show respect through your body language, even when you don't always feel like it (Robichaud, 2019):

Consider the Impact of Your Body Language

You have probably experienced times when you are extremely sweet and catering to your husband. Then, there are other times when you struggle to remain consistent with the same level of respect. Do you roll your eyes when you don't want to hear what he has to say? Do you cross your arms, pout, and give him the silent treatment for a few days? When he is trying to talk to you, do you ignore him and look away in defiance like a petulant child? All of these are nonverbal forms of disrespect.

Try to avoid eye-rolling by stopping to consider what he is saying to you before dismissing it as useless. The same goes for crossing your arms and looking away when he is trying to communicate with you. Be willing to take accountability and correction when needed.

Be Gentle in Spirit

Gentleness, grace, and humility are spiritual traits that emanate in everything you say and do. Above all else, this is what really speaks to your husband's heart. Having a gentle spirit is synonymous with being soft and submissive to your husband, which is what God desires from you in your marriage.

If you have grown accustomed to being rebellious, defiant, and disrespectful to your husband, then it may be time to apply the scripture from 1 Peter 3:3-4 to your life: "Whose adorning let it not be that outward adorning of plaiting the hair, and of wearing of gold, or of putting on of apparel; But let it be the hidden man of the heart, in that which is not corruptible, even the ornament of a meek and quiet spirit, which is in the sight of God of great price" (King James Bible Online, 1611c).

Give Him Your Full Attention

As a wife, your mind can easily be pulled in 10 different ways at once—between work, bills, children, and household chores—there seems to be no end to the multitasking. But when your husband is speaking to you, you should do your very best to lay aside all other distractions. Nothing should take precedence at that moment (except if the house is on fire, of course). Let him know through deep eye contact and fronting that you are completely invested in his words. Make it clear, too, that you're not just listening but also understanding, remembering, and applying what he tells you.

Smile at Him Often

Your genuine and effortless smile creates happiness in your environment, and that happiness spreads to your husband and your children both. In particular, your smile communicates to your husband that you are delighted to be in his presence and that you are eager to please him. It can also be seen as an inviting gesture, which can be used as a form of seduction to hint at your sexual advances.

Reciprocate Physical Responses

Your body language is probably most effectively communicated in response to your husband's romantic gestures. According to

Southern Productions, your response—or lack thereof—to your husband's sexual suggestions has a lasting effect on his self-confidence, and as a result, his success at work or in business. Do you slap his hand away when he tries to caress you? Or turn your back when he tries to hug you or cuddle with you in bed? When he's in the mood, do you make excuses so that you don't meet his sexual needs?

If you've been guilty of these actions in the past, then you should stop and reciprocate his romantic interests. Your reciprocation reminds him that his efforts aren't one-sided and also shows that you respect him.

Give Him Goodbye Kisses

Your husband shouldn't have to remind you to show your love and respect to him. If he's leaving for work in the morning and you respect the fact that he's going out to provide for you and your children, show your appreciation by kissing him goodbye. Doing this shows your love, support, and respect for him. Studies have actually proven that men who are kissed every morning before leaving for work are more successful than men who are not. A man who is respected and supported at home is more likely to be respected and valued at his place of business.

Cook His Favorite Meals

One of the best ways to show thoughtfulness toward your husband is by cooking his favorite meal. Let's say your husband likes his chicken fried, but the rest of the family likes their chicken baked. You can cater to his preferences by preparing fried chicken at least two or three times a week, just for him. By showing special consideration to his food preferences, you're making it obvious that he's high on your priority list.

Dress to Impress Him

Your desire to please your husband in every way includes the way you choose to dress, both at home and in public. Without saying anything, the way you take care of your appearance and wear garments that he finds flattering says that you respect yourself and are eager to please your husband. Putting effort into keeping yourself physically attractive also communicates to your husband that you want him to continue desiring you all the time.

Keep the Household Clean

Nothing says that you respect yourself, your husband, and your family more than keeping a tidy living space. To the best of your abilities, try to keep the home tidy. An orderly and tidy home leads to a peaceful environment where there is structure and standard. Your husband will love and cherish you for making an effort to keep things clean because most men can't function in disarray. Also, you're teaching your children the value of cleanliness, a trait that will be needed as they grow older.

Admire Him

This is another nonverbal language that goes back to your eyes—admiration. Praising him and showering him with verbal compliments is always appreciated, but taking a moment to look at your husband in a way that screams "respect," "appreciation," and "I'm so glad you're in my life" does something to a man that words can't describe. He'll know just by looking at you that you think the world of him and will in turn love you even more for recognizing his value.

Willingly Follow His Lead

Another telltale sign of respect shown through nonverbal communication is your willingness to follow your husband's lead. This may also tie into the topic of submission, but your body language won't lie when it comes to this. Your husband will easily be able to pick up on this because it will be reflected in your response time, your facial expression, and your zeal to do what was asked of you. Two heads can't rule a family, and neither can a body function optimally with two heads. This isn't to say that there aren't times when you can suggest ideas or offer a different perspective to your husband's leadership. Ultimately, though, being a dutiful wife will take you much further than being a stubborn, rebellious, and argumentative one.

Elevating Your Husband

The body language that's displayed between you and your husband speaks volumes about the true nature of your relationship. Once you understand the different types of body language and what they mean, you can begin using them with your husband, if you haven't been already doing so subconsciously.

According to Marriage.com, the various types of nonverbal communication styles include facial expressions, eye contact, personal space, paralinguistics, and appearance, to name a few (Smith, 2020).

Most of the body language cues are unambiguous and done subconsciously, so you can use the following signs to gauge your husband's level of interest, as well as your own:

1. **Smile constantly.**

A smile is generally seen as a positive facial expression, and because it appears on a part of your body that's the most revealing—your face—it conveys so much about what you're feeling within. Think about if you bought someone a gift, and when asked if they were pleased with it, they said yes but never smiled. You would be led to believe that they weren't being genuine.

People also tend to make judgments quickly about someone's emotional state and personality based on their facial expressions alone. Indeed, studies have shown that slightly raising your eyebrows and cracking a smile is synonymous with friendliness and confidence. When smiling frequently with your husband, it communicates that you feel safe, secure, and at ease in his company. Smiling also gives off an air of excitement and anticipation. The point is, your smile could be the outward expression of a sea of underlying emotions.

2. **Mimic his mannerisms (mirroring).**

Now, I mentioned mirroring earlier as a way of showing respect using nonverbal communication. Similarly, mimicking your partner's behavior also signals that you are deeply in love with him and find him very attractive, so much so that you want to do everything just like him. It's been said that imitation is the best form of flattery, so imitating your partner is, essentially, a way of saying that you're smitten!

Mirroring also occurs as a result of spending a lot of time together with someone. And so mimicking your husband's moves, temperament, and speech pattern all signify that the two of you are in love. It also shows that you are comfortable with following his lead, which further validates his status as a leader.

3. Lean into each other.

This is probably another subconscious form of body language you've already put to use. Either way, leaning into your husband is another sign of genuine interest, and so you should make the effort often. This doesn't only have to be when the two of you are in a conversation; when you're walking or standing together, you may seem to be drawn to him magnetically and begin leaning in. Also, leaning your head on his arm or his chest in public translates your feelings of trust and closeness with him. So, whether you're watching a movie together or waiting in a long line at a store, leaning your head on his shoulder is a beautiful depiction of your feminine nature and his stable, masculine, dependable strength.

4. Walk in sync.

Similar to mirroring, walking in sync with your husband is an overt revelation of the closeness and intimacy you share. When you match the pace of someone you love, it shows that you're in tune with them, or at least trying to be. Oftentimes, the more aware and in tune you are with your husband's nonverbal cues, the easier it will be to walk in synchronization with them.

5. Touch frequently.

Have you ever heard someone describe a couple by saying, "Those two can't keep their hands off of each other!" Well, that can be taken literally, because people who find each other attractive have an inclination to frequently and spontaneously touch one another. It's an instinctive action that you're probably doing without realizing, whether it's by fixing your husband's clothes in public, removing a strand of hair from his face, or hooking your arm into his as you walk. Frequent touching is often a sign of intimacy.

Besides what I've mentioned above, there are a few other nonverbal cues that indicate intimacy and an emotional connection between two people. The nonverbal signs listed are seen as more credible than verbal compliments and often outweigh spoken words if the body language communicates something different.

In the exact same way, your body language cannot be faked—if you genuinely love your husband, it's going to come through physically. Of course, you can also apply these nonverbal communication styles to your husband as well to see what his true feelings are toward you.

Other nonverbal cues that communicate intimacy between two people include things like wedding rings, matching tattoos, or matching outfits. For example, wearing your wedding ring and presenting yourself as a committed wife can have a positive impact on your husband's status and significance in society, because marriage is still seen as a milestone reserved for grown folks.

Furthermore, you can also communicate intimacy with your husband by sharing the same drinking glass, holding hands in public, kissing on the lips, and caressing intimate areas of each other's bodies like the upper arms, neck, waist, and back area. Engaging in these behaviors openly with your husband also lets the world know how serious your relationship status is.

Strengthening the Hierarchical Aspect of Respect in Marriage

Most of our houses are decorated with family photos, each of which tends to showcase different poses that we display, each for a different purpose. Some photos convey a serious atmosphere, some are funny, and still some others can convey respect. Curious about this last category? Indeed—photos that are meant to communicate respect through body language require an entirely different set of poses, and as you may have guessed, are an excellent thing to include in your home.

Remember, though, that as I give you an example of this kind of pose, I'm not trying to make you change the way you've been taking family photos in general. Take them, frame them, and place them around the house as you normally would. Think of this "respect pose photo" as an experiment that will give you a personal visual example of how your body language can convey respect to your husband. What you're doing here is making use of your husband's dominant frame in order to establish that hierarchical idea of respect we discussed earlier.

What you'll do is take a photo in which your husband is squarely in front of the camera, while your body is turned toward him with your arms wrapped around his waist or neck. This position should make it easy for your gaze to be upon him. Don't kiss him, flirt with him, or do anything to make the photo more cutesy. Simply look up at him and admire his strength, courage, and everything else about him that inspires your admiration. Take a few of those photos to see how they come out, and then choose the best one to frame and add to the decor around your house.

Moving on from photography, another universal method of demonstrating hierarchical respect through body language is bowing. When you think of bowing to someone else, I'm sure certain cultures come to mind. But even Western countries like the US know that one should bow in the presence of royalty, almost instinctually. And so bowing, across all cultures, really, is recognized as a gesture of respect.

That being said, let me clarify that I'm not suggesting you bow before your husband whenever he enters a room. However, what you *can* do is incorporate this concept in little, more subtle ways in your daily life, without making it seem like you're trying to literally kiss the ground he walks on. For example, you could try kneeling on the floor next to him while he's sitting on the couch. This way, instead of sitting next to him, you're communicating a height difference, and as such, placing him in a dominant position.

Keeping this couch idea in mind, if the two of you are snacking while watching TV, you could sit in front of him, using the coffee table to eat your snack, while he sits back on the couch. Keep in mind that you should sit close enough to him so that you're touching—your back against his legs, for instance. If he has no idea what you're doing, sitting close enough to touch will allow him to make the subconscious connection in his brain. Now, this doesn't have to be done for the entire duration of a movie or anything, but incorporating this method for at least a few minutes each day can truly cultivate a habit of respect being demonstrated by you to your husband.

One last area wherein this kneeling method is extremely effective is during your intimate time together. Your physical intimacy in the bedroom is a time when you're both in a vulnerable state, being completely exposed before one another. So, take this to heart: A wife in her naked, vulnerable state kneeling before her husband, being not only willing to be exposed but kneeling at his feet, is the ultimate show of reverence And as such, it is all but guaranteed to build him up in a powerful way.

With the knowledge of how your body language can be used to show respect to your husband, we're now ready to move on to Chapter 9, where we'll explore the importance of not interrupting your husband in public and how doing so can dislodge him from social standing as a leader.

Chapter 9:
Don't Interrupt and Correct Him in Public

As I've said before, the best marriages are formed through first being friends. Truly, when you're friends first, you enter into a marriage where you and your husband can be considered best friends. As such, you probably interact with each other at home in a very open, informal, and vulnerable manner. This is wonderful in the home, of course, but now, let's dive into this chapter's topic: conduct *outside* of the home.

When you are out in public together, you're going to be interacting with people who don't have access to the same level of friendship you have with your husband. Therefore, he is going to relate to them differently from the way he relates to you at home, which is completely natural. After all, they don't experience the same level of vulnerability that you do with him. And this becomes obvious when you consider how loving and attentive he is with you compared to others.

And so, out in public, your husband might portray a more stern, stoic demeanor. This doesn't mean he has multiple personalities or anything—what it simply means is that he's conducting himself based on the context. Since he is in a different environment, around people who are in different places in the hierarchy, he must conduct himself differently than what you're used to at home. That's all there is to it.

When you notice this shift in his demeanor, it isn't a green flag for you to undermine him by saying something like, "Oh, stop it, honey. Lighten up! Of course he'll be fine with it!" Sure, he may be fine with this kind of conduct from you at home, but that doesn't mean that same conduct is fitting for interactions in the public sphere, with people outside your marriage. So, by making statements like this, you might be unknowingly shifting his social standing among his friends and acquaintances. How, exactly? By equating it to the same standing he has with you.

Furthermore, you need to be especially careful with your choice of words, manner of speech, and overall attitude when dealing with your husband out in public. Try to understand that if he is acting differently with a friend, acquaintance, or family member than he does with you, you should take it as a compliment to the special dynamic the two of you share in your relationship. However, never assume that he wants to extend the treatment he gives you to everyone else. Your closeness with him is what sets your relationship apart from the rest, and so you should handle that privilege with care.

That being said, we're now going to go over some things you should cease doing to your spouse in public, according to iMom (Mark Merril, 2015). If you have already adopted these habits and mannerisms, it may be encouraging disrespect from others outside of your relationship, while at the same time bringing harm to your marriage:

1. Don't criticize your spouse to others.

Criticizing your husband to others damages his reputation and, by extension, your marriage. It also dampens whatever respect others may have had for you, seeing that you are so willing to speak negatively about your life partner in such an open way. In short, you come across as an untrustworthy person. It also communicates to outsiders that your marriage isn't a safe place for your spouse to be in either.

2. **Don't make your husband the butt of the joke.**

Belittling your husband, especially when out in public, sends the message that you don't care about his feelings, even if you claim to. If you're consistently making him the punch line of every joke, and encourage others to do the same, he may begin to wonder if they really are just jokes.

3. **Don't treat your husband like a child.**

You and your husband are both adults, which means that neither of you should be treating the other like a child. If you're in public with your husband and you speak down to him and order him around like a child, think of the message that conveys to other men and women. They will automatically lose respect for him, and begin treating him the same way you have. And when they no longer see him as a man that you actually respect, they will also begin to disrespect *you*. Treating a grown man like a child is humiliating and is never a good idea.

4. **Don't constantly correct and challenge your husband.**

When your spouse is offering details about a particular topic or recounting a past event, try to resist the urge to interrupt him with your own input or correct perceived mistakes. This is also a way of belittling him, and it digs away at his confidence. If you truly want to be of assistance to him, look for opportunities to honor him in public, like allowing him to speak freely without the threat of your interference.

5. **Don't share the intimate details of your love life with others.**

Now, this is something that both husbands and wives are guilty of. But as a wife, speaking negatively about your husband's sexual performance—and any other aspects of your intimate moments—can be seen as a breach of trust. If your husband suddenly isn't performing in the bedroom as he used to, discuss it with him directly and look for a solution together instead of opting to reveal such sensitive information to friends and family.

6. **Stop flaunting your body to the world.**

The present culture in our world tends toward superficiality, and as such, it simply does not value the sanctity of modesty. With everyone looking for validation on social media, attention has become the new currency, and many women are willing to flaunt their physical features to others, whether by posting suggestive photos online or dressing inappropriately in public. And doing this as a wife is particularly dangerous, as it advertises her as being available to others, even if that isn't her intent. Point being, dressing modestly is always a sound choice. It communicates that you are only available to your husband because, as a wife, that is the only person you should be available to.

Social Dynamics in Public Settings

There are many things you may be doing as a wife that you think are helpful or create balance, when in reality, they actually work to undermine your husband. Ultimately, your marriage is supposed to be a partnership, wherein you share the same goals with your spouse, understand the same vision, share the same opinions, and work together with him as a unit.

But while these ideal marriage expectations are the goals many of us aspire to, the human element often gets in the way, making us prone to disagreements and different points of view. This, then, can lead to you undermining your husband, which negatively affects your marriage, family life, and social life. As I've stated, it can display itself in behaviors such as correcting your partner, sharing his faults and personal challenges with others, or purposefully going against the rules he has already established for the children.

And again, worst of all, most of your undermining behavior is likely being done in front of others, which can begin to erode the foundation of your marriage. According to Fatherly, here are some of the common ways you're probably undermining your husband's public demeanor without knowing it, and why it's crucial to put a stop to them:

When Disciplining Your Children

As I alluded to previously, two heads cannot effectively run a household—this only tends to chaos and confusion. Furthermore, this is one area in particular where you should avoid undermining your husband's leadership. When your husband has already set certain ground rules and boundaries for the children, it is counterproductive to work against the system of order he has already established in an attempt to be favored by the kids. It only leads to disharmony.

As a result, your children will start seeing him as the bad guy for setting a bunch of rules that *you* disagree with. This creates a "split" that leads the children to do whatever they want, believing that the rules set down for them are faulty, and so they're better off finding their own way.

In order to prevent this disorder from taking place, there are some key things that can be seen to. Clinical social worker Jan Carey suggests that both should parents come together to create a list of five rules These five rules can be openly discussed in hopes of reaching a common goal regarding what each rule is meant to achieve. By discussing each rule, you and your husband will each gain clarity on why enforcing them will be beneficial for the children, and most importantly, it will prevent one parent from ever undermining the other.

When Maneuvering In-Law Relationships

Oftentimes, it's found that one spouse in a marriage comes from a tightly-knit family structure prior to being married. And this can actually cause friction at times when it comes to pleasing their spouse and extended family. What often happens is that, because of those close familial bonds, one spouse may end up putting the needs of their extended family above their partner.

If this were to characterize your husband, for instance, it would likely leave you feeling isolated and unprotected, possibly provoking you to lash out at him. You might not understand how your husband could possibly prioritize anyone over you. After all, he has left his parents' home and has started a life of his own. Well, in order to avoid such a compromising situation, you need to sit down with him and boldly discuss where you draw the line in regard to your needs versus the needs of his family.

When Discussing Family Finances

Financial woes are one of the biggest stressors in marriage, as well as one of the biggest causes of divorce. Unsurprisingly, this is also one of the main areas in which couples undermine each other. Again, when it comes to family finances, both you and your husband need to be on one accord. That can of course be challenging, though, especially when you both have a different understanding of the value of money.

For example, if you grew up in a family that lacked financial resources, you may now feel the need to overcompensate as a money-making adult by purchasing expensive, useless things that give off the illusion of security. Regardless of how lavish some of these purchases might be, this is actually a poverty mindset. Your husband may want to invest the money into more meaningful things, like life insurance, building a home, saving for your children's future, or starting a business.

While the opposite could be just as possible, let's just say, for instance, that you're the partner who would rather spend money frivolously. In this case, your spending habits could be undermining your husband's attempts to spend the money wisely. This, then, is a clear sign of disrespect.

When Discussing Sex and Intimacy

After the initial honeymoon phase, it's normal for the frequency of sex to undergo some changes. To put it plainly, you and your husband are "doing life" together now, and with pressures such as work, children, and housekeeping, there are many things distracting your ability to connect sexually in the ways you once did.

Sadly, what often happens—especially in our age of technology—is that these external pressures cause us to turn away from the comforts of our spouse in favor of other, lesser comforts, such as social media. Indeed, the comforting distraction of social media can take up the time and interest that you should be giving to your husband in the form of sex. This can then, of course, lead to him feeling undermined and undervalued, as though everything else is more important to you than your desire to be intimate with him.

To prevent these feelings from arising, try engaging in new and abstract activities together—things that are foreign to both of you. If neither of you has ever taken a painting class or a salsa lesson, you can do it together to reignite the same feelings of curiosity and discovery that you had when you first began seeing each other. Being in the moment together once again is a surefire way to spark intimate feelings once again.

Enhancing Respectful Communication

Alright, now that we've covered some of the many ways your behavior could be showing disrespect to your husband, we're going to counteract that. Below, we're going to look at a new list of strategies for maintaining respect and support for your husband in social settings, according to Mom Junction. Take the time to consider some of these positive behavioral traits:

1. **Cherish his advice.**

Men, by nature, feel their best when they feel valuable, which is why they enjoy fixing things. So, when the two of you are at home or out shopping, involve him in your decision-making process. This shows him—and others— that you value his opinions and suggestions. However, you shouldn't force him to make decisions for you. Keep your discussion on topics such as finances, your children's education, your future living locations, and things of that nature.

2. Take note of his preferences.

When you have taken his advice, be sure to take a mental note of his preferences for the future. This will demonstrate your thoughtfulness for the next time you're in a similar situation, as you'll know exactly what his choices are. This is also an example of putting him first and, by doing so, he won't feel like he's being undermined.

3. Offer open compliments.

The antithesis of being critical and belittling your husband is paying him sincere compliments—both in public and in private. Of course, your compliments will go a long way when they're given in public, so when you're having a discussion with your friends or family and his name comes up, be sure to highlight his good qualities. That being said, be wary not to do it in an obnoxious way that could upset or annoy other people in the group.

4. Verbalize your admiration of him.

Your husband seeks your admiration and appreciation as a form of motivation to keep working toward your goals, but if you keep that admiration to yourself, it does little to encourage him. So, don't be shy about letting him know how much you admire his dedication as a husband and a father.

5. Don't criticize him in front of others.

It should go without saying that this is one of the most offensive and disrespectful things you can do to your husband. By insulting him or criticizing his words or actions in front of others, it invites others to disrespect him as well. Instead, talk to him privately—and respectfully—to let him know where you think he went wrong and what you think he could have adjusted.

Now, before jumping over to the final chapter, I want to offer a bit more detail on the dangers of being too critical in your relationship, and how refraining from this behavior can lead to a stronger and healthier marriage.

Firstly, understand that no one likes being around an overly critical person because well, they tend to suck the life and positivity out of every situation. Think of how that critical boss at work made you feel when you knew you were putting your best foot forward, but nothing seemed to satisfy them. I'm sure you wished for a better boss or thought of leaving the job to escape their critical nature, right?

Well, that's exactly how your husband feels when you constantly criticize him. According to Dr. Jessica Higgins, being too critical in a relationship can lead to a toxic dynamic, and furthermore, it erodes any positive feelings in the relationship over time (M, 2017).

Constant criticism toward your partner can actually destroy the union altogether and, on top of that, is recognized as a major predictor of divorce. Criticism focuses on passing judgment on your partner's flaws and is often expressed through disapproving, critiquing, blaming, and nitpicking. The bottom line here is that there's nothing constructive or inspiring about it, as it only centers on attacking the negative aspects of someone's character.

So, as we prepare to enter Chapter 10, take this to heart: If you cherish your marriage and want to save it, put an end to criticizing your husband There's only so much character assassination a man can take, be it to his face or behind his back.

Chapter 10:
Adorn Yourself for Him

Believe it or not, the way in which you adorn yourself says a lot about the way you honor your husband. Just as the lesser light of the moon shines because it reflects the light of the sun, you also reflect on your husband when you step outside into the public sphere. And according to Wives of Jannah, honoring your husband should actually be the only reason for you to get truly dolled up (Wyatt, 2018).

Now, some women get dressed up for their husbands, but with the wrong motive. They follow the fashion trends of the women they see in public or on television because they want to ensure that they're captivating their husband's attention before his eye lingers over to any other women out there. So, in actuality, this method of dressing up is coming from a place of insecurity.

Instead of trying to compete for his attention with the countless other women in the world, you should simply dress up for him because it's a way of *honoring* him. When you shift your focus from doing it to compete with others to doing it for your husband, it makes all the difference in the world. In fact, when he knows that you've touched up your makeup, styled your hair, or put on that perfectly fitted dress just for him, he will appreciate and love you even more for it.

Women have a tendency to disparage themselves, but the truth is that one of the main reasons your husband decided to marry you was most likely because he thought you were gorgeous. You are the apple of his eye, really—he was probably smitten with you from the first day he laid eyes on you. Even though you're a few years older now and have possibly even packed on a few extra pounds, rest assured that he still finds you as beautiful as the first day you met. It certainly doesn't hurt, of course, if your inner beauty complements your outer beauty. And that can come through—you guessed it—through showing respect.

Now, without a doubt, your husband probably has a preference when it comes to the clothes you wear. You may wear outfits that he thinks make you look like a snack, and at the same time, you probably also have some clothes he's not too fond of. If you feel stuck and don't know what to wear, all you have to do is ask him. And once you're aware of what his favorite style of clothing is for you, don't be afraid to wear it more often.

When he notices your effort to dress more to his liking, he will appreciate the time and preparation you put into each occasion. As the saying goes, "It's the thought that counts." When your husband sees that you took the time to do something out of the ordinary for him, the gesture will warm his heart and cause his passion to burn for you even stronger.

Desiring to Please Your Husband

Your looks carry more weight in your marriage than you may realize. While they don't account for all of your husband's attraction to you, they were definitely a defining factor in the beginning stages of the relationship.

Surely, your husband was attracted to other qualities about you, like having a sense of humor, being kind, demonstrating values and principles, and having hobbies. However, attraction certainly helps—and as such, our focus now will be on physical adornment.

According to Psych Central, on average, men tend to rate physical attractiveness as a requirement for a mate more than women do in regard to the men they pursue (Washington, 2021). While this may be true, physical attraction isn't the only requirement a man considers when deeming a woman "attractive." Indeed, your husband may have also been looking at your personal style, hygiene, posture, and thoughtfulness—not to mention your values and principles.

Other factors play a role, too, like your waist-to-hip ratio and the way your curves protrude in the clothes you wear These very well could have hooked him when you first met, too. Besides playing into your physical attractiveness, these features are also telling of your level of fertility. To some, this may seem like a shallow point, but ultimately, it's in a man's primal instincts to be attracted to physical attributes that point to child-bearing.

And if your husband ever told you that the moment he saw you it was "love at first sight," this can actually be understood as a strong physical attraction that he had toward you, which is the same as, well, sexual attraction itself. That being said, sexual attraction and romantic attraction are distinct from each other, meaning that you can love someone romantically without being sexually attracted to them. In most cases, though, sexual attraction precedes romantic attraction, which is most likely what first attracted your husband to you.

So, in essence, your physical appearance mattered to your husband when you two first met, and you can be certain that it still matters to him today.

Building Attraction and Connection

You might not remember what you wore when you first met your husband, but I'll bet he remembers it perfectly! Perhaps you wore a particular dress that hugged your physique in all the right areas, or maybe the color of the outfit really accentuated the color of your eyes. Whatever it was, you wore it boldly and confidently, and your husband seized the moment. With that in mind, not only would he be the best person to let you know what you were wearing then, but he would know exactly what you should wear to catch his eye today.

The truth is, you are what you wear. And in the realm of nonverbal language, the way you dress communicates more than you might realize. We often hear the idiom, "Don't judge a book by its cover," but we inadvertently judge others every day based on their dress code, don't we?

And so, the same applies to you—the way you choose to dress can say a lot about your identity. For example, dress scholars Mary Ellen Roach and Joanne Reicher believe that dressing is one of the ways by which we send social signals, according to Science of People (Van Edwards, 2016). Roach and Reicher state that your clothing conveys the following:

- how powerful you are
- how influential you are
- your level of intelligence
- your financial bracket
- your social status

People also create first impressions about you based on what you wear, whether that's a positive or a negative first impression. Besides the dress, style, and fit of your clothes, the colors you choose to wear also communicate a lot about you, and can even affect your behavior. Here's a guide to what some of the colors mean and how the ones you choose to wear may even be affecting your behavior:

- **Blue:** loyalty, tranquility stability
- **Red:** passion, aggression, intensity
- **Yellow:** happiness, optimism, youth
- **Green:** healing, hope, success
- **Black:** power, mystery, professionalism
- **White:** purity, cleanliness, innocence

Of course, these are just some of the colors and their meanings. If you're trying to evoke a certain mood from your husband through your dress, this knowledge is definitely useful. But colors are only a small factor in the game of attraction. People's perception of you is also dictated by how you tailor your clothes to fit you, how you style your outfit, and your brand preference.

Even on regular occasions like going to the grocery store, you may tend to dress up. But when you opt for these occasions, you're essentially dressing up for strangers who pass you by. It would be more worthwhile if you put that same effort into looking good for the man who loves you, wouldn't you agree?

And if your husband is gushing over the way you present yourself, rest assured that other men are doing the same. When you begin to dress for the occasion, whether it be more formal, professional, casual, or edgy, you'll begin to turn heads effortlessly.

When you're going out to an event where your husband's friends are going to be, you can have fun being eye candy at the gathering. You're not going to be doing this in a flirtatious and seductive way, obviously—and I'm certainly not advocating for women to sexualize themselves in front of others to make their husbands feel better—but being the beautiful, elegant, committed woman at your man's side grants him status among his friends and even among business associates. In fact, his friends and business partners will also love and respect him even more when they see how attractive his wife is!

And with our final chapter concluded, that just leaves the Conclusion, where we'll ruminate over what we've learned over the past 10 chapters.

Conclusion

And just like that, we've come to the end of *10 Ways to Show Respect to Your Husband*, and I can say with confidence that I know if you've gotten this far, you must have picked up some nuggets of knowledge along the way. The goal of all of this, as I'm sure you know, has simply been to give you the wisdom and understanding you need to navigate your marriage effectively.

You are now equipped with everything you need to know when it comes to *respecting* your husband—and not just loving him. After all, he is the one called to love you. Once you both understand the uniqueness of your individual roles, it makes fulfilling each other's needs much easier.

So, let's recap a few of the most outstanding ways we've covered on this journey of showing respect to your husband. Firstly, we discussed allowing him to parent the children without your intervention as something that should not be compromised. The children you share together deserve the right to experience their father in the fullness of his masculinity in the same way they've gotten a chance to experience you as their mother—without intervention.

Next, we covered the need to speak well of your husband to others, whether that be family, friends, associates, or his own children. Remember that you represent your husband by the way you speak of him. And as you now know, you're also giving those you speak to a preview of your own character by default. So, speaking well of him reflects positively on you, and on the contrary, speaking negatively of him reflects poorly on you as well. Truly, the worst thing you can do as a mother is discuss your husband in a negative light in the presence of your children.

Moving on, we faced the fact that your marriage predates your children and, as such, needs to remain your priority over them. While it may seem logical and at times convenient to invest more in your children, neglecting your marriage will ultimately leave you feeling empty and disconnected from your husband—especially once the kids have moved out.

As you now know, romance novels have proven to be a source of unrealistic expectations and idealistic fantasies that lead to the destruction of many marriages. With the statistics showing that the majority of readers are women, the argument is being made that the "emotional porn" of these books influences the minds of readers just as badly as actual pornography watched by many men today. If women require their husbands to stop watching pornography because of its neurological effects, then they must also ditch their romance novels.

Of course, the other pressing issues we've gone over in this book can't be overlooked, and these included putting family above your career, respecting his method of provision, using your body language to show respect, prioritizing time for him over household chores, resisting the urge to correct him in public, and adorning yourself for him. Whether all or just some of these points apply to you, it's more than worthwhile to take the time to account for your actions and consider where in your marriage you could start demonstrating more respect to your loving husband.

When all is said and done, a wife must understand that respect for her husband is not an option if she wants the marriage to work—it's a command from God. And if you genuinely fear God and want your marriage to be an example of His goodness, there is an order you must follow that requires respect from you to your husband. So, practice these methods of respect, bask in the goodness of your marriage—and all that your husband has provided it—and watch as your beautiful union sets an example for others!

References

Ackerman, C. E. (2017, February 28). *What is gratitude and why is it so important?* Positive Psychology. https://positivepsychology.com/gratitude-appreciation/

Arbuckle, B. (2020, March 10). *How respecting your husband can make him a better leader at home.* Focus on the Family. https://www.focusonthefamily.com/marriage/how-respecting-your-husband-can-make-him-a-better-leader-at-home/

Ayeni-Bepo, A. (2023). *How to prioritize your spouse in your marriage.* Overcomers Counseling. https://overcomewithus.com/couples/how-to-prioritize-your-spouse-in-your-marriage#:~:text=When%20you%20prioritize%20your%20marriage

Babbar, K. (2015, July 30). *Use non-verbal communication to give and receive respect.* Www.linkedin.com. https://www.linkedin.com/pulse/use-non-verbal-communication-give-receive-respect-khyati-gupta/

Bush, S. (2016, August 12). *The Parenting Gender Gap: The different ways men and women parent.* HuffPost. https://www.huffpost.com/entry/the-parenting-gender-gap_b_11430888#:~:text=Nurture%20vs%20Discipline

161

Cait. (2020, December 24). *4 ways i help my husband lead me*. Mrs. Midwest. https://www.mrsmidwest.com/post/4-ways-i-help-my-husband-lead-me#:~:text=Give%20him%20space%20to%20make

Connolly Counseling Center. (2017, July 6). *Parenting differences between men and women*. Connolly Counselling Centre. https://www.counsellor.ie/parenting-differences-men-and-women/

COPH Staff. (2016, September 8). *"If you want to go fast, go alone, if you want to go far, go together". African Proverb - Martha Goedert*. News & Events. https://blog.unmc.edu/publichealth/2016/09/08/if-you-want-to-go-fast-go-alone-if-you-want-to-go-far-go-together-african-proverb-martha-goedert/

Dawson. (2017, August 17). *Speaking well of your spouse, reflects well on you!* Mike and Susan Dawson. https://mikeandsusandawson.com/speaking-well-spouse-reflects-well/#:~:text=When%20you%20consistently%20speak%20well

Diaz, J. (2023, January 22). *Link: 40+ romance novel sales statistics [2023]*. Sweet Savage Flame. https://sweetsavageflame.com/link-40-romance-novel-readers-and-sales-statistics-2023/#:~:text=Who%20reads%20romance%20novels%3F

Doyle, E. (2019, September 28). *How to speak well of your spouse in public all the time*. ChurchLeaders. https://churchleaders.com/outreach-

162

missions/outreach-missions-articles/359953-how-to-speak-well-of-your-spouse-in-public-all-the-time.html

Hyatt, M. (2016, February 12). *Why speaking well of your spouse is so important*. Full Focus. https://fullfocus.co/why-speaking-well-of-your-spouse-is-so-important/

Jamal, H. (2022, December 31). *How to balance work and family life in marriage*. Hello, Love. https://medium.com/hello-love/how-to-balance-work-and-family-life-in-marriage-698e0e2eba7c

King James Bible Online. (1611a). *1 Corinthians Chapter 7 KJV*. Www.kingjamesbibleonline.org. https://www.kingjamesbibleonline.org/1-Corinthians-Chapter-7/#4

King James Bible Online. (1611b). *1 Corinthians Chapter 15 KJV*. Www.kingjamesbibleonline.org. https://www.kingjamesbibleonline.org/1-Corinthians-Chapter-15/#33

King James Bible Online. (1611c). *1 Peter Chapter 3 KJV*. Www.kingjamesbibleonline.org. https://www.kingjamesbibleonline.org/1-Peter-Chapter-3/#3

King James Bible Online. (1611d). *2 Peter Chapter 1 KJV*. Www.kingjamesbibleonline.org. https://www.kingjamesbibleonline.org/2-Peter-Chapter-1/#3

King James Bible Online. (1611e). *Ecclesiastes 4:9 KJV "Two are better than one; because they have a good reward for their labour."* Www.kingjamesbibleonline.org.

https://www.kingjamesbibleonline.org/Ecclesiastes-4-9/

King James Bible Online. (1611f). *Ecclesiastes Chapter 4 KJV.* Www.kingjamesbibleonline.org. https://www.kingjamesbibleonline.org/Ecclesiastes-Chapter-4/#9

King James Bible Online. (1611g). *Ephesians Chapter 5 KJV.* Www.kingjamesbibleonline.org. https://www.kingjamesbibleonline.org/Ephesians-Chapter-5/#25

King James Bible Online. (1611h). *Genesis Chapter 2 KJV.* Www.kingjamesbibleonline.org. https://www.kingjamesbibleonline.org/Genesis-Chapter-2/#24

King James Bible Online. (1611i). *Genesis Chapter 2 KJV.* Www.kingjamesbibleonline.org. https://www.kingjamesbibleonline.org/Genesis-Chapter-2/#18

King James Bible Online. (1611j). *Mark 10:8 KJV "And they twain shall be one flesh: so then they are no more twain, but one flesh."* Www.kingjamesbibleonline.org. https://www.kingjamesbibleonline.org/Mark-10-8/

King James Bible Online. (1611k). *Matthew Chapter 12 KJV.* Www.kingjamesbibleonline.org. https://www.kingjamesbibleonline.org/Matthew-Chapter-12/#34

King James Bible Online. (1611l). *Proverbs 15:1 KJV "A soft answer turneth away wrath: but grievous words stir up anger."*

Www.kingjamesbibleonline.org. https://www.kingjamesbibleonline.org/Proverbs-15-1/

King James Bible Online. (1611m). *Proverbs 18:21 KJV "Death and life are in the power of the tongue: and they that love it shall eat the fruit thereof."* Www.kingjamesbibleonline.org. https://www.kingjamesbibleonline.org/Proverbs-18-21/

King James Bible Online. (1611n). *Proverbs Chapter 10 KJV.* Www.kingjamesbibleonline.org. https://www.kingjamesbibleonline.org/Proverbs-Chapter-10/#19

Kowalski, K. (2020, September 14). *Porn addiction: Worse than cocaine?* Medium. https://katya398.medium.com/porn-addiction-worse-than-cocaine-fad644594cd5

Les. (2017, June 21). *Why criticism poisons happy marriages - SYMBIS assessment.* SYMBIS Assessment. https://www.symbis.com/blog/not-criticism-poisons-happy-marriages/

Liu, C. (2014, March 11). *Liu: Romance novels, like porn, yield unrealistic expectations.* Iowa State Daily. https://iowastatedaily.com/108655/opinion/liu-romance-novels-like-porn-yield-unrealistic-expectations/#:~:text=In%20both%20scenarios%2C%20there%20is

M, K. (2017, August 24). *How to show respect to your husband: 13 basic things to try.* MomJunction. https://www.momjunction.com/articles/how-to-respect-your-husband_00430461/

Mackler, C. (2018, March 20). *5 easy ways to communicate better in your relationship*. One Love Foundation. https://www.joinonelove.org/learn/5-easy-ways-to-communicate-better-in-your-relationships/

Mark Merril. (2015, August 28). *7 things you should stop doing to your spouse in public - iMOM*. IMOM. https://www.imom.com/7-things-stop-doing-to-spouse-public/

Maul, D. (2022, September 19). *6 reasons to put your marriage before your kids*. All pro Dad. https://www.allprodad.com/why-your-spouse-should-come-first/

Pace, R. (2020, November 16). *20 things a couple can do to strengthen a marriage*. Marriage Advice - Expert Marriage Tips & Advice. https://www.marriage.com/advice/relationship/things-couple-can-do-to-strengthen-a-marriage/

Robichaud, J. (2019, October 22). *9 ways to show respect to your husband*. Radiant Marriage. https://www.radiantmarriage.com/9-ways-to-show-respect-to-your-husband/

Smith, S. (2020, November 12). *What your body language says about your relationship*. Marriage Advice - Expert Marriage Tips & Advice. https://www.marriage.com/advice/relationship/what-your-body-language-says-about-your-relationship/

Smith, S., & LeSuesur, J. (2023). *Pornography use among young adults in the United States*. Ballard Brief.

https://ballardbrief.byu.edu/issue-briefs/pornography-use-among-young-adults-in-the-united-states#:~:text=Key%20Takeaways%2B-

southernproductions. (2013, September 17). *25 ways to communicate respect to your husband.* Southern Productions Mississippi Wedding Planner and Florist. https://southernproductions.net/2013/09/25-ways-to-communicate-respect-to-your-husband/

Sriram, R. (2020, June 24). *Why ages 2-7 matter so much for brain development.* Edutopia. https://www.edutopia.org/article/why-ages-2-7-matter-so-much-brain-development/

Starcher, J. (2018, January 11). *15 things wives should stop doing.* FamilyLife®. https://www.familylife.com/articles/topics/marriage/staying-married/wives/15-things-wives-should-stop-doing/

Team, E. (2022, May 12). *How to balance parenting responsibilities with your spouse | Minno Kids.* Www.gominno.com. https://www.gominno.com/parents/how-to-balance-parenting-responsibilities-with-your-spouse/

Timesofindia.com. (2023, June 30). Unrealistic expectations. *The Times of India.* https://timesofindia.indiatimes.com/life-style/relationships/love-sex/how-do-romance-novels-affect-real-life-relationships/photostory/101391689.cms?picid=1013 91840

Washington, N. (2021, August 20). *How much do looks really matter in a relationship?* Psych Central. https://psychcentral.com/blog/do-looks-matter-in-a-relationship#love-vs-physical-attraction

Wyatt, M. (2018, January 9). *Real reasons to dress up for your husband • Wives Of Jannah*. Wives of Jannah. https://wivesofjannah.com/soul-care/the-real-reason-to-dress-up-for-your-husband/#:~:text=I%20dress%20for%20him%2C%20or

Young, K. (2015, February 9). *Relationships: The 6 reasons people leave (and how to avoid it happening to yours)*. Hey Sigmund. https://www.heysigmund.com/6-reasons-people-leave-relationships-and-how-to-avoid-it-happening-to-yours/

Made in United States
Orlando, FL
04 June 2024